Things That Are (Said), and Things That Are Not
A brief look at the ideological context
of the Basque language

Basque Literature Series No. 15

Things That Are (Said), and Things That Are Not

A brief look at the ideological context of the Basque language

Naroa Anabitarte

Center for Basque Studies
University of Nevada, Reno
2022

Library of Congress Cataloging-in-Publication Data

Names:
Anabitarte, Naroa, author.
Title: Things that are (said), and things that are not : a brief look at the ideological context of the Basque language / Naroa Anabitarte.

Other titles: Things that are said, and things that are not
Description: Reno : Center for Basque Studies Press; University of Nevada, [2022] | Includes bibliographical references.

Summary: "The aim of this book is to present an overview of the ideological context of the Basque language. Ideas about language emerge in conjunction with ideas about other areas such as politics and science. For this reason, we have focused on the link between language and national ideologies. We have also included some reflections on the rhetoric used in scientific research on the Basque language as well as on the individualism-collectivism controversy so central to the social sciences. Finally, given the dynamic nature of ideologies, we also studied the evolution of the discourses on the Basque language, with a particular emphasis on silenced discourses"--Provided by publisher.

Identifiers: LCCN 2022030030 | ISBN 9781949805697 (paperback)
Subjects: LCSH: Basque language--Rhetoric. | Basque language--Psychological aspects. | Basque language--Social aspects. | National characteristics, Basque. | Group identity--Spain--País Vasco.

Classification: LCC PH5135 .A53 2022 | DDC 499/.92--dc23/eng/20220727
LC record available at https://lccn.loc.gov/2022030030

Contents

0. Introduction 7

1. Towards a rhetorical ideology of the Basque language 11

2. Language awareness, ideology, and rhetoric . 19

3. Attitudes towards the Basque language and the context of the controversy . . . 29

4. Language and nation 41

5. The discursive complexity of Basque nationalism 57

6. The people of the Basque language? . . . 73

7. Basque language and scientific debates . . 87

8. The rhetorical dimension of ethnolinguistic vitality 99

9. The evolution of discourse 113

10. Things which are not (said) 125

References 155

0. Introduction

Beautiful songbird,
where are you singing?
The wind carries the crying of the stones
through the valleys of Zaraitzu.
Benito Lertxundi. *To the Bard of Itzaltzu.*

We Basques love our language and do not hold back when it comes to expressing this love. Indeed, we have made many sacrifices for it throughout our history. Perhaps the most moving yet brutal story about this love of the Basque language is that of the bard of Itzaltzu, recounted by Arturo Campion at the beginning of the twentieth century (Campion, 1923). The hero Gartxot is sent to prison for murdering his son, Mikelot. He serves out his sentence at Elkorreta (a mountainous area above Itzaltzu, Navarre), where, with pigeon crumbs as his only sustenance, he slowly starves to death.

The story featured in a song recorded by Benito Lertxundi in 1981 ("Itzaltzuko Bardoari" from Altabizkar) and in a film directed by Asisko Urmeneta and Juanjo Elordi in 2011 (Gartxot. Konkista aitzineko konkista; Gartxot. The conquest before the conquest) and has become very popular in recent years.

The tale of the Bard of Itzaltzu chronicles an event that took place almost a thousand years ago. Passed on orally, it contains certain anachronisms which Campion rightly points out. Indeed, several versions of the story exist. Campion first heard it when he was staying with the Berrade family in Itzaltzu where he used to go hunting every year. It was told to him by the youngest daughter of the family, Andresa, but was not the only version he was familiar with. Campion said that while most of them were very similar, the one that resonated most with him was told to him by a hundred-year-old woman. This version was also the one that coincided most with records found in the church of Orreaga (Roncesvalles) and the Archives of Navarre. According to this version, Gartxot was punished for murdering his son Mikelot whom the monks at Roncesvalles wanted to recruit as a singer. Impressed by the quality of his voice, the monks wanted to teach the young boy to sing in Latin instead of Basque, which they expressly forbade. The monks were known for entertaining passing pilgrims with renditions of Turoldus's "Song of Roland," an epic account of the battle of Roncevaux (Orreaga) in which Charlemagne is depicted as a hero. Young Mikelot, however, considered Charlemagne an enemy of the Basques, and his father, who would have preferred to see his son dead than hear him singing in Latin, kills him to protect him from the monks. This is the version narrated in the 2011 film—a violent and moving love story about a father and son and the Basque language.

Love is an ideological construct, and the ideological dimension of love has frequently been examined from a feminist perspective. The study of romantic love has shown the harsh consequences that the ideological construct can entail. The love of a language can also invite reflection. Love for a language—I believe—is a socially constructed process rather than something that is felt on an individual level. I understand the psychological processes, ideas, and opinions about languages as intertwined with sociological processes—in other words, in a context of ideologies.

This premise is what I try to explain in this work. The reader will find some basic ideas for a psychosocial study of Basque. I put forward these ideas as the starting point for more in-depth research. In this short book, my aim has been to reflect on the ideological context of the Basque language from a social psychology and rhetorical perspective.

In the first chapter I discuss the presence of rhetoric in all areas of life and underline its importance in understanding identity and language.

The second chapter deals with the concept of language awareness. The ideological dimension of the concept is emphasized, and it is presented as a process that takes place in a socio-historical context. From this perspective, ideas about language are presented as ideas within an ideological context.

Similarly, the third chapter reflects on attitudes to languages. This section discusses the interpretations derived from treating motivation and attitudes as individual psychological phenomena, in the field of social psychology in general, and in Basque sociolinguistics in particular. I stress the importance of understanding attitudes and motivations in their rhetorical context when studying Basque sociolinguistics.

The following chapters explain the ideological context of the Basque language. In the fourth chapter, language and nation, and the connection between them is discussed. I also examine the links between language and national ideologies. In the fifth chapter I reflect on the complex discursive production of the ideology of the Basque nation. I also underline the challenges of analyzing the discourse in specific Basque language contexts. I reveal the paradoxes we found in Basque nationalist discourse and discuss the inherent difficulty of the term "nationalist discourse."

In the sixth chapter, I examine individualist and collectivist ideologies, and reflect on their impact on Basque language ideology.

Academic issues are explored in the following two chapters. The seventh chapter examines the interaction between scientific debate and commonsense ideas related to the history of the language, arguing that scientific debate does not take place outside society; while, in the eighth, I reflect on the concept of ethnolinguistic vitality used by academics in the field of Basque sociolinguistics (Giles, Bourhis & Taylor, 1977).

In chapters nine and ten, things that are not said take center stage. In discourse analysis, what is said and what is not said is highly significant, and this is discussed in the two chapters. In chapter nine, I examine the evolution and changes in the discourses on the Basque language that have taken place over time, and include several examples. I use a key landmark in Basque sociolinguistics (the years of the Franco dictatorship) to discuss the subject of opacity/transparency of controversy throughout this chapter. In the tenth chapter, I examine what is not said in the discourse on the Basque language. I explain the importance of what is (left) unsaid in the construction of the Basque language. An example of this is the analysis of what is said and what is not said during the most important national improvised poetry (bertsolaritza) competition (Txapelketa Nagusia), an event that takes place every four years.

In the last chapter I discuss the conclusions that can be drawn from this book. I deal with the rhetoric of rhetoric, reflecting on the uncertainty that postmodern and deconstructionist thinking entails.

1. Towards a rhetorical ideology of the Basque language

In exactly the same way, you are not a pack of neurons; you are what your own pack of neurons collectively do. And if I want to touch your "self," I must do so by word and deed that, once they leave me, become a part of you.
T. E. Feinberg. *From Axons to Identity.*

In 2009 I defended my doctoral thesis, having spent many hours in the lab peering down an electron microscope in the hope of identifying the exact location of a number of proteins linked to Alzheimer's disease. Back then, my reading focused on the molecular aspect of memory, but as I became more interested in ideology and rhetoric, I discovered Michael Billig's fascinating rhetorical approach to social psychology and was hooked. I stopped searching for gold-marked proteins and threw myself into the academic world of discourse and rhetoric.

Although the two fields may seem worlds apart, I have essentially been working on the same subject for all these years. Identity and identity-related issues have always fascinated me and have guided my career. That being said, I still feel I need to justify my journey from molecules to rhetoric as current boundaries between disciplines and subdisciplines are so restrictive.

When I wrote my dissertation, my understanding was that Alzheimer's disease caused a loss of several types of memory, and along with it, the loss of identity. In Western culture, hegemonic discursive practices have constructed dementia as a "loss of self," and people with dementia are often seen as "empty shells" (Guendouzi and Müller, 2006; Hamilton, 2008). Both academic and non-academic discourses on Alzheimer's disease and dementia tend to shape our view of people with the disorder (Guendouzi and Müller, 2006). Researchers who have highlighted the social dimension of Alzheimer's disease have introduced a new perspective on the subject, and, by focusing on the language used in social interaction with Alzheimer patients, have redefined identity, memory, and the disease itself:

> In all of this work, Alzheimer's disease is approached as a human issue within multiple linguistic and social contexts, rather than exclusively as a slowly progressive disease of the brain. (Hamilton, 2008, p. 92)

One study conducted along such lines involved the moving case of a South African woman named Deborah Brodie (Ridge, Makoni & Ridge, 2003). In the study, the authors analyzed the process of Brodie's diagnosis with Alzheimer's disease. By changing their perspective on the condition, they managed to transcend the pathological deficit perspective and explore the implications of retained ability by examining the evolution of her speech and comparing the personal and scientific writings of her youth with those she had written since her diagnosis. In addition to written texts, they also examined her speech and the discourse of the practitioners and others involved in her care. The fascinating study takes its title from the devastating statement made by Brodie herself when faced with her disability: "I want to be like a human again." These findings have profound implications for the treatment of patients with dementia:

> We have attempted to evoke and reflect on the reality of DB as a person: someone attempting to continue engaging the world in the face of unpredictable failures in her repertoire of communicative and cognitive strategies. This social enterprise becomes visible and significant when we move from framing her dementia as an entity, and understand it rather as a process. (Ridge, Makoni & Ridge, 2003, p. 167)

Different approaches to the study of Alzheimer's disease and the discourses that surround it construct both the disease and the concept of identity (Guendouzi and Müller, 2006). At the same time, Deborah Brodie's and similar cases reveal the centrality of discourse in the process of constructing a person's identity. Similarly, Giedre Zickyte and Maite Alberdi's film *Yo no soy de aquí* (*I'm not from here*) examines the process of constructing the identity of a Basque emigrant to Chile named Josebe, showing how she continues to build her identity through her discourse. When studying Alzheimer's disease, therefore, the ideology of the disorder must also be closely examined by carrying out a critical analysis of the discourse in the literature on the subject (Fairclough, 1992). How Alzheimer's disease and the processes involved in developing and losing memory are constructed through discourse is a topic of great interest. Several researchers have described the content and process of memory itself as social rather than individual actions (Edwards and Middleton, 1988; Middleton and Edwards, 1990a; Vygotsky, 1929; Wertsch, 1987). Context and discourse should therefore be at the heart of any study on processes of memory and forgetfulness.

This leads us into the sphere of rhetoric. And once we enter the world of rhetoric, we realize that it is impossible to leave. The discipline of rhetoric, which thrived from the era of the classical Greek thinkers until the advent of Descartes, has been enjoying a revival in different fields—known as the "rhetorical turn" (Simons, 1990b)—since the middle of the last century. As Simons states, "there is no escape from rhetoric" (Simons, 1990b). Rhetoric is found in all areas of research; therefore, any study ostensibly carried out from a neutral or objective perspective is also subject to examination from a rhetorical perspective:

> *The Rhetorical Turn* is one among many recent works to counterpose rhetorical perspectives on inquiry against the dominant objectivist presuppositions of our age. (Simons, 1990a, p. 1)

So, once we manage to grasp the omnipresence of rhetoric, we realize that even the study of molecules in a laboratory starts from a rhetorical standpoint. Rhetorical perspectives and discourses on memory condition the design of laboratory experiments and therefore impact their results (Wolpaw, 2002). In the words of Jack and Appelbaum:

> Research in neurorhetorics should be two-sided: not only should researchers question the neuroscience of rhetoric (the brain functions related to persuasion and argument), but they should also inquire into the rhetoric of neuroscience (how neuroscience research findings are framed rhetorically). (Jack & Appelbaum, 2010, p.411)

Related to this, as memory—at least explicit memory (Tulving, 1972)—and identity are socially constructed processes, we come up against the problem of studying social phenomena in the laboratory. Although we can study the dynamics of molecules using laboratory techniques, it is impossible for us to measure the social dimension of the dynamics of these molecules. We cannot reproduce human sociality in all its nuances in the laboratory. In the field of social psychology, there have been many in-depth reflections on the limitations of experimental techniques for calibrating the dynamics of social phenomena such as identity and memory. As Billig wrote in one of his articles, there are several issues that experimental techniques cannot address:

> However, the objects, which these scientists [cognitive scientists] study, are intrinsically unobservable. No high-powered microscope or techniques of neural imaging will be able to identify a mental representation or a cognitive categorization. These are not material objects that, in principle, could be viewed if we had the right equipment. (Billig, 2009)

This critique is directed at the dominant position of the cognitivist view in the field of psychology. In fact, the cognitive approach has prevailed in social psychology in recent decades. The cognitive approach emerged in opposition to the current known as "behaviorism" and the emphasis shifted from the study of behavior to the examination of the internal structures of mind.

The cognitive approach has become the dominant perspective in psychology in general (Rumelhart, 1980). According to it, language itself is understood to be a reflection of internal mental states. Faced with this, psychologists who analyze discourse have reacted by rhetorically questioning such foundations. These researchers do not see language as a reflection of mental states: "they have argued against the very idea of treating language-behaviour as if it is a sign for the real, underlying psychological entities" (Billig, 2009).

So the critique of the cognitive approach to psychology has been much more profound than a critique at a methodological level, in that the very assumptions used by cognitive psychologists have been fundamentally questioned. From a cognitive point of view, it is understood that the brain/mind processes information which it receives from the exterior, which is why the aim of cognitive scientists is to examine how this process takes place. Moreover, from a cognitive point of view, we store mental representations of the outside world in our human brain/mind, which is why we are able to understand and interpret external stimuli. It has been these basic assumptions in cognitive science that have been criticized from a discursive perspective (Billig, 2009).

It is important to note, however, that there are a number of differences among the different lines of discursive research (Fairclough, 1992; McKinlay and McVittie, 2008). That said, researchers who take a discursive approach agree on one principle: language is action. Therefore, what people do through their discourses is examined by looking at discourse itself (Potter and Wetherell, 1987; Howitt, 2010; McKinlay and McVittie, 2008). The development of the social constructionist view of discourse analysis initiated by Jonathan Potter and Margaret Wetherell (Potter and Wetherell, 1987) is sometimes identified as the Loughborough School of Discourse Analysis, since a substantial group of researchers have developed their research under the DARG (the Discourse and Rhetoric Group) umbrella (Howitt, 2010). Derek Edwards, a DARG member, portrays the core of their work as follows:

> Common to us all at that time was a concern with how psychology's standard way of dealing with thought and understanding, as products and processes of individual mentality, could be approached in an alternative way through an examination of talk and text, and shown to be intrinsically, and not just peripherally or additionally or derivatively, social. (Edwards, 2012, p. 425)

From this perspective, Michael Billig has addressed the path of rhetorical psychology, and has made important contributions to social psychology and the social sciences in general, stating that rhetoric refers primarily to reasoning, basically meaning argument or argumentation (Billig, 1987; Howitt, 2010). The link between discourse and rhetoric is natural "since they share a focus on language as social action and as doing things" (Howitt, 2010, p. 200). Billig's work is central to the field of rhetorical psychology. According to him, rhetoric is not limited to the discourse used by specialized speakers; we find rhetoric intrinsically within any discourse. It is not understood as a gift that some special people have, but in a broader sense:

> As a result, a knowledge of rhetoric provides more than knowledge of the specialized, professional tricks of the orator. It also can throw light upon ordinary modes of thinking. (Billig, 1987, p. 193)

Because discourse analysis allows us to analyze psychological processes such as human thought, identity, and attitudes in their rhetorical context, I have turned my attention from internal processes in the brain to language by focusing on different types of discourse:

> The discursive analyst does not search for unobservable inner schemata that determine outward utterances, but examines the details of the utterances in their interactional and rhetorical contexts. This is not to deny that internal states and inner experiences exist. It is just that these are methodologically always just out of reach. (Billig, 2009)

As I am concerned with Basque identity, and taking into account the centrality of the Basque language in the construction of this identity, I have offered some reflections on the language in the following pages. My aim was to examine what and how we think about the Basque language. I wanted to focus on its ideological context, so this book examines the ideological processes of the construction and deconstruction of the Basque language from a psycho-social point of view. In the same way discourses on Alzheimer's disease construct the disease itself, I argue that discourses on Basque are responsible for constructing the language itself. I have drawn heavily on the rhetorical approach to social psychology so elegantly studied by Michael Billig. Rhetoric being both a resource and an object of research (as Michael Billig has said), I examine the rhetoric of discourses on the Basque language rhetorically.

2. Language awareness, ideology, and rhetoric

To a major degree, philosophy is an adult attempt to deal with the genuinely baffling questions of childhood.
G. B. Matthews. *The philosophy of childhood.*

Michael Tomasello and his fellow researchers at the Max Planck Institute have compared human sociality to the sociality of chimpanzees in numerous studies (Tomasello, 1999; Tomasello, Dweck, Silk, Skyrms & Spelke, 2009). In their research, which was carried out from an evolutionary psychology perspective, they were seeking the answer to the question "What makes us human?" In a book on the origins of human communication, Tomasello discusses language (Tomasello, 2010). He argues that the skills of shared intentionality developed by humans during evolution are at the core of language and communication in general. He defends the idea that it is this basic ability that distinguishes us from other animals:

> Linguistic acts are social acts that one person intentionally directs to another. . . . These acts work only if the participants are both equipped with a psychological infrastructure of skills and motivations of shared intentionality evolved to facilitate interactions with others in collaborative activities. Language, or better linguistic communication, is thus not any kind of object, formal or otherwise; rather it is a form of social action constituted by social conventions for achieving social ends, premised on at least some

> shared understandings and shared purposes among users. (Tomasello, 2010, p. 343)

He argues that human communication—and culture in general—differs qualitatively—as well as quantitatively—from the communication skills of other animals, and is generally developed in conjunction with the skills and motivations required for shared intentionality. In terms of core competencies, he emphasizes the human capacity for "recursive mind-reading" and argues that the basic motives for shared intentionality are "helping" and "sharing" (Tomasello, 2010).

Human-developed communication is cooperative, and it is more complex than the intentional communication of some other primates because the underlying ability is qualitatively different. The underlying sociocognitive infrastructure, in addition to the ability to understand the intentionality of individuals, has enabled shared competencies and motivations.

In addition to encountering these competencies at the core of human communication, he argues that languages, too, derive from the same basic sociocognitive infrastructure developed in evolution:

> "Arbitrary" communicative conventions, including linguistic conventions, rely on the same cooperative infrastructure as "natural" human gestures, and indeed they derive originally from these natural gestures through a "drift to the arbitrary." (Tomasello, 2010, p. 322)

According to Tomasello's research, human communication is an action that is carried out cooperatively, and the subject of this action is the plural "we." This places the socio-cognitive capacity to act as "us" at the heart of all institutionalized human behavior. The plural subject is, then, basic to language and other institutions (Tomasello, 1999). Paradoxically, the cognitive ability to construct an "us" in cooperation has also built differentiated "us" groups during evolution:

> Such group-mindedness in cooperation is, perhaps ironically, a major cause of strife and suffering in the world today. The solution – more easily described than attained – is to find new ways to define the group. (Tomasello, 2009, p. 100)

The universal capacity for creating "us" groups during evolution led to the construction of particular "us" groups. Equipped with a universal sociocognitive capacity for communication through language, humanity constructed and continues to construct particular languages. When Tomasello suggests that we should find new ways to define the group as a solution to humankind's multiple sufferings, he is referring to the rhetorical dimension of particular "us" groups. Although the ability to engage in a "plural subject" is a universal psychological characteristic of humans, the "us" groups constructed are differentiated ones which are situated historically, both in terms of languages and other institutions. As Michael Billig mentions in his book *Ideology and Opinions*, in social sciences, concepts can be universal or particular:

> In the social sciences, concepts can be distinguished as being universal or particular. Universal concepts denote phenomena which are presumed to occur universally, regardless of historical epoch or type of society. (Billig, 1991, p. 59)

The human capacity to institutionalize behavior is universal, but institutions which are created are particular and time-specific. Although basic competence in language or communication is a universal phenomenon, languages are time-specific, particular phenomena.

Not only does humanity have the ability to construct "us" groups, but it also has the ability to think reflexively about these groups' characteristics. Accordingly, we construct discourses about these "us" characteristics. It is precisely through these discourses that "we" are constructed. With regard to languages and the basis for communication, we humans speak about and discuss languages, in that way constructing them. In this sense languages are ideological constructs.

In various research projects on languages, the concept of *language awareness* has been used. Numerous works have been published on the subject which is often connected with multilingual models of education. Some of the research has focused on how bilingual or multilingual children develop *language awareness* (Arnberg and Arnberg, 1992). In today's world, the topic under discussion is how nation states manage different languages in education (Liddicoat and Taylor-Leech, 2015). In this context, many researchers, rather than viewing language as an isolated "object," have developed the concept of *culture awareness* alongside the concept of *language awareness*, thus understanding language as a part of culture. The importance of embedding translations from one language into another in the cultural context is emphasized from this perspective. When learning a new language, it is essential to take into account your own cultural context and that of the language you are learning, according to these researchers (Byram, 1997; Byram, 2012). All this research shows us that we do indeed think about languages. Apart from speaking them, we talk about them, and build discourses around them.

As children grow, they acquire language and develop *language awareness,* but this process takes place in a specific context. So rather than being understood as a universal psychological process, in this book I consider language awareness to be a specific phenomenon. I do not believe awareness of the existence and nature of language to be a universal psychological process; I think of it rather as a process that takes place socially and in a particular context. In the same way, Billig, for example, draws a distinction between the language awareness we have developed since the emergence of nationalisms from the language awareness that would have existed at other times:

> Humans might have spoken from the dawn of history, with mutually unintelligible ways of talking being developed in different places, but this does not mean that people have thought of themselves as speaking "a language." The concept of "a language"—at least in the sense which appears so banally obvious to "us"—may itself be an invented permanence, developed during the age of the nation-state. (Billig, 1995, p. 30)

The era of nation-states led to specific classifications of different languages, identifying which ones "qualify" for inclusion in the "language" category and which ones do not (and should be considered "dialects"). Referring to pre-modern times, Billig states:

> To put the matter crudely: the mediaeval peasant spoke, but the modern person cannot merely

> speak; we have to speak something – a language. (Billig, 1995, p. 31)

So nowadays we speak languages (or dialects), and we are aware of the fact. We have language awareness in the sense that we know we speak something. Along with that, and because we know that we speak something, we also talk about that something. We have discourses about language. And we build languages through these discourses (beyond the specific language code that we are using).

As children acquire a language in their own contexts, they not only become aware of the existence of different languages with regard to phonology and so on: they also receive ideas about the languages. Which ones are considered languages and which ones are not. They receive ideas about where and where not to speak languages, and learn about hierarchies among languages. They receive discourses about languages.

So, when dealing with languages, we encounter ideologies. When I say that there are ideologies about languages, I do not mean that there is a coherent corpus of ideas about a specific language, because I understand that ideology is a social process that is dynamic, changeable, and contradictory. As can be seen in the work of researchers on the ideology of languages, different authors work on the concept of ideology from multiple personal perspectives, with each one emphasizing different aspects. In the book *Language ideology*, for example (Schieffelin, Woolard & Kroskrity, 1998), different perspectives are reflected in the contribution of the different authors. But as Woolard mentions in the introduction, above and beyond all their differences of opinion, these authors all agree on one point:

> In spite of the many possible points of divergence, the essays gathered here share a fundamental emphasis on the social origins of thought and representation, on their roots in or responsiveness to the experience of a particular social position. Seeking to bring out the social dimensions of cultural conceptualizations of language, most contributors go further, insisting on the tie of cultural conceptions to social power as the crucial feature of the phenomena under study, although power is variously conceived. (Woolard, 1998, p. 10)

The *thinking society* analyzed by Moscovici shares this point of view. Moscovici understands that the origin and development of human thought is conditioned by social contexts (Moscovici, 1984). He refers to the social origin of thought. The argument that everyday thought processes are ideological processes has even been made from the rhetorical psychology perspective. Following Billig's example, I have placed everyday opinions and attitudes about the Basque language within an ideological context. In his work, Billig examines the link between individuals' thought and ideology:

> The processes of everyday thinking can be processes of "ideology." This means studying thinking and the holding of opinions, in its wider social context. . . . In ordinary thinking, people use a "common sense," which they do not themselves invent but which has a history. (Billig, 1991, p. 1)

As mentioned above, from a rhetorical point of view ideology is not taken to be a coherent, stable corpus of ideas. On the contrary, it is a dynamic, contradictory social process. This is how I too understand ideologies that may exist with regard to language, in this particular case to Basque. They are dynamic sets of ideas which are changeable and contradictory, and I understand them to be embedded in power relations. People do not reproduce ideologies in the same way they receive them, and this dynamic process in itself makes ideologies contradictory and changeable. People receive language ideologies in the process of socialization, and, using rhetorical thinking, "discuss" the "common sense" ideas they receive, thus developing ideas about language through discussion:

> The ordinary person—the subject of ideology—is not a blind dupe, whose mind has been filled by outside forces and who reacts unthinkingly. The subject of ideology is a rhetorical being who thinks and argues with ideology. (Billig, 1991, p. 2)

If ideologies about languages exist and if we talk and think about them, then discourses about languages have a rhetorical dimension. The ideologies we receive about languages are rhetorical; and at the same time people, through rhetorical thinking, construct opinions about them in a dynamic way:

> At the core of this approach lies the connection between arguing and thinking. In the rhetorical approach, the thinker is seen as a debater, engaged in argument either silently with the self, or more noisily with others. (Billig, 1991, p. 31)

From the point of view of psychology, in order to study social phenomena such as that of the Basque language, it is very important to pay attention to the rhetorical dimension of human thought. According to Billig, in many studies cognitive psychologists view thinking as "problem solving," and, in such studies, in general, the finite result problems posed by experimental psychologists do not reflect the problems we face on a daily basis. The internal or external debates we may have about languages do not have finite result "solutions." They are potentially infinite discussions, just as with discussions on other social issues:

> However, the vast majority of everyday problems which perplex people in ordinary life, possess no such finite structure. For instance, the problems of ethics, of politics, of assessing the character of others, of deciding what to do with our own lives, possess no such definable end-point which can be reached by correct deduction. (Billig, 1991, p. 39)

So, many of the problems we have on a daily basis and the problems of logic are different in nature. Thoughts about our identities are rhetorical in nature. They do not have one single, correct result as in a math exercise. Billig analyzes the psychological implications of Protagoras's famous maxim "in every question, there are two sides to the argument, exactly opposite to each other":

> The saying draws attention to the human capacity for critical thinking, which is based on the faculty for negation. We possess the capability to resist arguments by inventing the counter-arguments which constitute the inevitable other side to each question. (Billig, 1991, p. 47)

The rhetorical approach, therefore, presents psychosocial processes (such as the construction of the Basque language and Basque identity) as rhetorical debates between ideology and thinking. Rhetorical ideologies "accumulated" throughout history, formed by arguments and counter-arguments, are products of the rhetorical thoughts of transitory, changing individuals and groups in interaction with them. Ideology, psychology, and rhetoric are intertwined:

> It can be assumed that the ways of thinking, which are created by and within ideology, are themselves inherently rhetorical. Similarly, the use of rhetoric will itself reflect the patternings of ideology. In this way, the problems of ideology, psychology and rhetoric are interlinked. (Billig, 1991, p. 3)

For all these reasons, I felt it important to examine Basque sociolinguistics and the construction of identity from a qualitative social psychology perspective. Therefore, I have left quantitative studies to one side, preferring instead to turn our attention to the rhetoric of Basque language ideologies and power relations among them.

3. Attitudes towards the Basque language and the context of the controversy

The person who professes support for democracy or female equality, but who acts or speaks in undemocratic or discriminatory ways when it comes to specific situations, is no artefact.
M. Billig. *Arguing and Thinking.*

My father has often repeated a story about my grandfather. With pride and admiration, he told us how his father used to react when his sisters—my aunts who were quite young at the time—would arrive home speaking Spanish, clearly contaminated by the outside world. He never told them off, he simply ignored them. Once they realized they would not get his attention if they spoke Spanish, they switched to Basque, and my grandfather would calmly join in the conversation again.

I have heard this story from my father many times. He hardly even knew my grandfather who died in a workplace accident when my father was four or five. He was a barrel maker and worked in a factory in the town of Pasaia on the coast of Gipuzkoa. He drove a nail through his leg and died within days as there were no cures for tetanus at the time. His death had a huge impact on the whole family and my grandmother had to make some tough decisions. My father, who was still very young at the time, was sent to boarding school in Zaragoza (Spain). Two maiden aunts of his were nuns there, so it was decided that he should go away to school. He spent ten years there, returning home only in the summer. If his father had been there to see it, he would have felt great sadness. Like the boy in *Gartxot. Konkista aitzineko konkista* (Gartxot. The conquest before the conquest), the child from Pasaia had gone to Zaragoza and returned without his language; they had deprived him of his mother tongue, replacing it with Spanish. During the summer holidays, however, my grandmother would send him to stay with some relatives on a farm in Goiatz (an agricultural village in Gipuzkoa where Basque is spoken daily) so he could get his native language back.

When my parents met, my mother had just started learning Basque. She grew up in Tolosa (an inland town in Gipuzkoa where Basque was mostly outlawed at the time), but although her father was a native Basque speaker, her mother was from a town in Navarre called Mañeru where Basque had fallen into disuse and did not speak the language, so Spanish was spoken at home. It seems that my great-grandfather, who had moved to Mañeru from Otsagi (a village in the north of Navarre in the Pyrenees), spoke Basque but, although he moved in nationalist circles, did not pass the language on to his children.

So, while my mother did not learn Basque from an early age, she says she was familiar with some songs and it was spoken around her. She was born in my great-grandparents' house in Tolosa and spent her childhood there. My great-grandmother was also Basque and spoke the language. When my mother finished school, she became a social worker. Early on in her career, something happened that spurred her on to learn Basque. She was visiting a woman on her deathbed who had a daughter with Down's syndrome. She says it was a very difficult situation: the Basque woman could hardly speak Spanish and was trying her best to communicate with my mother. With her last breath, the woman was trying to explain how she wanted her daughter to be cared for after her death. Deeply affected by the situation, my mother immediately went off and started learning Basque and my parents decided that their children would be Basque speakers too.

In one way or another, similar stories are repeated in every family, generation after generation. Everyone in the Basque Country feels something about the Basque language. This "attitude towards the language" is something that has survived the passage of time. In fact, there is nothing new about Basques having an attitude towards the language.

In the field of social psychology, the concept of attitude has been central, and a lot of research focuses on attitudes and changes in attitudes. The concept itself is not understood by all psychologists in the same way, and many different definitions exist (Billig, 1993; Fiske and Taylor, 2013; Fraser, 1994; Jaspars and Fraser, 1984). Although it is a highly complex concept, it is found very casually in everyday discourse:

> Although social psychologists have been much concerned to provide exact, and official-sounding, definitions of "attitude," the concept seems to be one of those which gives little trouble in everyday discourse. In everyday life, we take it for granted that we all have "attitudes." (Billig, 1987, p. 175)

If we consider it normal to have attitudes about different issues, when it comes to Basque, the situation is no different. Each of us considers the context we live in to be "normal," so it is sometimes difficult to question whether or not certain things are "normal."

Although social psychologists have failed to reach a consensus on the definition of attitude, there is one thing they all agree on:

> They [social psychologists] tend to agree about one aspect, which has important rhetorical implications. Attitudes refer to evaluations which are for or against things, issues, people or whatever. (Billig, 1987, p. 176)

So, for many social psychologists, the basic component of attitudes is their evaluative aspect (Albarracín and Vargas, 2010; Eagly and Chaiken, 2005; Ferguson and Fukukura, 2012). According to this view, the core component of attitudes is assessment, and stimuli are categorized through evaluative dimensions:

> Attitudes categorize a stimulus, a long and evaluative dimension. As such, attitudes broadly dispose people to respond positively or negatively, as inferred from their specific cognitive, affective, and behavioral responses. (Fiske & Taylor, 2013, p. 232)

An example of this might be attitudes towards racism. If a person favors racial diversity, they will have a positive assessment of different races—a positive attitude. Similarly, a person who opposes Christianity will have a negative attitude and evaluation of Christianity. In the same way, there have been positive and negative attitudes towards Basque throughout the history of the language, depending on the assessment that people made of it. Some people may be in favor of Basque, while others are against it. Supporters of the Basque language are often referred to as *euskaltzaleak* or Basque enthusiasts. To us Basques, Basque enthusiasts are a normal part of everyday life, but attitudes in favor of or against a language do not seem natural when they refer to other languages. We realize, thus, that attitudes towards languages are not so commonplace. In Germany, for example, the idea of some people being pro-German language and others being against it would be considered unusual today. In the Basque Country, slogans and images denoting attitudes towards the Basque language are displayed in many official and other buildings, such as Ikastolas (pro-Basque schools), shops, etc. Examples include the "Euskaraz Bizi" ("Live in Basque") slogan and the iconic Argitxo elf logo, which were originally created for a campaign launched by the Ikastola association in the 80s and can still be seen on the walls of many Ikastolas and other schools today. The extent to which this symbol has become well-known in Basque society is reflected in the book *Ikastola mugimendua. Dabilen herria*:

> Over all these years, thousands of students have been educated and raised with Argitxo thanks to the multitude of murals, stickers, puzzles, DVDs, and dolls found in all the Ikastolas. . . . Despite the fact that it was originally designed to promote the Euskaraz Bizi movement, the elf character transcended the initiative and has become a pro-Basque symbol throughout society. (Iza, 2010, p. 194)

Signs with "We speak Basque" and other similar messages have become part of the landscape, and many companies display the "Bai Euskarari" ("Yes to Basque") certificate. It would be virtually impossible to count all the pro-

Basque language initiatives, as many of them have become part of our everyday landscape (costumes, posters, etc.) and the songs have outlived successive generations.

Although it is less common nowadays, the "Euskal Herrian Euskaraz" ("Basque in the Basque Country") group still carries out "elimination days and weeks" when the Spanish or French names of towns on road signs in the Basque Country are painted over.

So, attitudes found in everyday conversation about the Basque language are also reflected in the physical landscape of the Basque Country.

The ideas about attitudes in many academic writings in the field of sociolinguistics (Echeverria, 2005; Lasagabaster, 2005; Lasagabaster and Sierra, 2009) and the sociolinguistic model of Basque in general are based on the positive/negative evaluation ideas found in social psychology. In her book *Notes on Basque Culture* (2019), Larraitz Ariznabarreta argues that the dominant discourse of Basque sociolinguistics is structured around several general principles. Among the principles she mentions is the idea of a positive attitude towards the language:

> In lieu of full linguistic proficiency, the mere positive attitude towards the language, and the functional use of some basic, modest structures is deemed enough by most. Significantly, the regional administration's campaign to encourage the use of Basque among non-speakers in 2008 literally stated: "A little bit means a lot." *From the tiny acorn grows the mighty oak*. (Ariznabarreta, 2019, p. 95)

Moreover, in this attitudes-based view, individuals' motivations take center stage, and the psychological motivations of individuals are not placed in a rhetorical context. On the contrary, they are understood to be internal psychological forces:

> This principle that regards language as a private matter and speakers as the eventual liable subjects for its survival, has, of course, implications on a personal and social level. The personal implication immediately suggests a question about which the intrinsic motivational forces that move an individual into learning a language are. (Ariznabarreta, 2019, p. 96)

As the sociolinguistics of Basque is structured around these ideas, stakeholders in the Basque language industry try to answer these motivational questions in order to take steps towards the normalization of the language. How can we make Basque attractive to people who do not know the language? How can young people who have learned Basque be motivated to speak it in their free time?

The problem with this view is that when motivation and attitudes are treated as individual psychological phenomena, human psychology differs from the context and, in particular, from the rhetorical context. If attitudes and motivations were individual characteristics of psychology, it would be difficult to understand why some of us have attitudes towards certain issues and not towards others. Attitudes are found in context, and so the contextualization of their analysis is of great importance:

> One aspect of the wider context, which is largely ignored by psychologists who concentrate upon the individual's motives, is the rhetorical or argumentative context of attitudes. (Billig, 1987, p. 176)

Like Billig, authors who have examined attitudes from other perspectives have also emphasized the social dimension that attitudes and social psychology have in general (Abric, 1984; Moscovici, 1963). All of these researchers criticize the trend toward individualism in social psychology from a cognitive perspective. Although they agree on this point, Billig underlines the rhetorical and argumentative nature of the social context, distinguishing himself from authors who place themselves in the theory of social representations (Billig, 1993; Moscovici, 1984).

People do not have attitudes to subjects at random. The existence of an attitude towards a language should lead us to think that language is situated in a controversial context. As mentioned above, when one looks at other languages around the world one immediately realizes that not all languages have an attitude towards them. The rhetorical context of Basque has nothing in common with the rhetorical contexts of many other languages, most of which are not considered controversial in context:

> Whether the topic is political, moral, religious, commercial, or whatever, an attitude refers to a stance on a matter of public debate and disagreement. (Billig, 1987, p. 177)

In a particular society and at a specific time, there may be attitudes about certain issues, while in other societies there may be no attitudes about them. And when times change in the same society, the attitudes do not necessarily have to be about the same issues. For example, just as there are attitudes towards Christianity in the Basque Country today, at other times Christianity was deeply rooted and there was no attitude towards it. Back then, you would never have heard "Happy Winter Solstice"—which implicitly criticizes Christianity in a rhetorical context—instead of "Merry Christmas." Nobody would have argued about whether it was better to have a St. John's Eve bonfire on the 21st of June instead of the 23rd, or whether or not it should even be called the "St. John's" bonfire. These were not topics of discussion, but, as times changed, when the dominant ideology of Christianity became a topic of discussion, attitudes about it began to emerge.

The concept of attitude must, therefore, be understood in a specific social context, and the social context of attitudes is controversy. Attitudes require controversy to be present:

> The controversial aspect of attitudes implies that not all beliefs are attitudes. Within a given society, there will be certain matters which are controversial, and others which are so obvious that no-one seriously questions them. About the latter sort of issue, one does not hold attitudes. (Billig, 1987, p. 177)

Returning to the subject of Basque, attitudes for or against it do not emerge because people find it appealing or unappealing, regardless of context. A paternalistic view of the language as a treasured object to be cared for—the idea that it needs to be treasured because it is old and special—has found its way into the Basque speakers' collective imagination. When singer Anje Duhalde sings "Love me less and enjoy me more" in his song *Etxekoandre*, he is criticizing this conceptualization of the Basque language. Contrary to the belief that these traits will touch the hearts of non-speakers as a motivational impulse to learn Basque, the idea I am presenting about attitudes deviates from such a point of view:

> The implication is that attitudes are more than visceral responses for or against a stimulus. They are stances on matters of public debate. That being so, the possession of an attitude indicates a statement of disagreement as much as of agreement, and it signifies an implicit willingness to enter into controversy. In consequence, we can expect the possessors of attitudes to justify their stances, to criticize competing views, and generally to argue about the issues. (Billig, 1987, p. 178)

Therefore, in order to examine the social psychology of attitudes towards the Basque language, I will move the focus away from each individual's particular motivations and, instead, approach the ideological context of the controversy.

At the beginning of this chapter, we saw attitudes towards the Basque language that connected several generations. My grandfather's silence when his daughters spoke Spanish was a reflection of his attitude towards the Basque language and identity. Through silence he paradoxically expressed his position in a controversial context, and through silence he sought to avoid the disruption of intergenerational language transmission. My other grandfather also interrupted language transmission through silence; he did not speak Basque to his children. My father's aunts in Zaragoza interrupted his language transmission by not uttering a single word to him in Basque. My mother and father, on the other hand, ensured the recovery and transmission of the Basque language with their attitude.

They were all individuals. If we had been able to talk to them, they would have justified their attitudes and criticized opposing attitudes, arguing the reasons for their opinions. It would be impossible to interpret their attitudes through a questionnaire that simply divides them into groups for or against Basque and analyzes the data. This would fail to take the rhetorical context into account. In fact, attitudes themselves would not exist without a controversial context:

> The criticisms and justifications form an integral part of the attitude, for, without the argumentative context, there would be no attitudes. (Billig, 1987, p. 178)

The idea is therefore clear: if there are attitudes towards Basque it is because the context that surrounds the language is controversial. However, in many public debates today identifying a controversial context cannot be done directly. As I will discuss in more detail in chapter 9, discourses and arguments on controversial issues change over time, along with the process of institutionalization/deinstitutionalization of a specific view of the issue. On the other hand, from a rhetorical point of view, attitudes are matters of great complexity:

> Attitudes are likewise best understood as temporary, context-dependent leanings on a given controversial issue, usually encompassing a range of positions – latitudes of acceptance in Sherif and Hovland's (1961) terms –and oftentimes a good deal of ambivalence. (Simons, 2014, p. 22)

Moreover, inconsistencies that may exist between a general attitude and private actions, from a rhetorical point of view, are not gaps that appear to us as the result of a particular methodology. Rather, inconsistencies are inherent to the rhetorical context.

4. Language and nation

Genealogy, in short, is first and foremost a way of thinking.
E. Zerubavel. *Ancestors & Relatives.*

In today's world of nations and nationalist ideology, discourses and ideologies about language are closely linked with national ideologies. As I mentioned in the chapter entitled "Language awareness, ideology and rhetoric," when it comes to classifying what a language is and what it is not, the criteria used are not usually exclusively linguistic. Haugen, for example, uncovered the limitations of purely linguistic criteria in his study of the complexity of the concepts of dialects and languages, and spoke of the links between languages and nations:

> In trying to clarify these relationships, linguistic science has only been moderately successful. Even in the Renaissance it was perfectly clear to serious students of the subject that the term "language" was associated with the rise of a nation to conscious unity and identity. (Haugen, 1966, p. 925)

In order to examine hierarchies between languages, the terms "language" and "dialect," and concepts such as "developed" and "underdeveloped" languages, Haugen attaches importance to the link between language and nation. He defines a nation as an effective unit for acting on the international political stage, and, because of the need for social unity in order to be more effective as a political unit, argues that the national idea calls for a single linguistic code (Haugen, 1966).

In the same way, in recent years several anthropologists have taken into account the ideological and political dimension of language in linguistic anthropology. In the introduction *Language Ideologies*, for example, Woolard mentions the origins of the link between nations and the ideology of languages:

> It is a truism that the equation of language and nation is not a natural fact but rather a historical, ideological construct. This construction is conventionally dated to late-eighteenth-century German Romanticism and Johann Herder's famous characterization of language as the genius of a people, and thus it is often referred to as the Romantic or Herderian concept of language. (Woolard, 1998, p. 16)

Although this conceptualization of language is called Romantic or Herderian, Woolard links it to the French Enlightenment and to the French philosopher Condillac. She explains that the nationalist ideology of language was exported through colonialism and is globally hegemonic today. As such, the development of the ideology of nationalism has been associated with ideologies about languages in many studies (Blommaert and Verschueren, 1998; Errington, 1998). In the nineteenth century, languages were conceptualized as "natural objects" linked to a culture, and combined with the political dimension, the idea of nations which has prevailed in today's world began to develop:

> The equation of one language with one culture was endowed with political significance: a linguistically united community ("nation"), when tied to a

> territory, could claim to deserve a state of its own. In effect, exactly because linguistic differences were seen to be independent of human social intention, they could serve as an apparently neutral warrant for political claims to territory and sovereignty. (Gal & Irvine, 1995, p. 968)

Jaqueline Urla's book *Reclaiming Basque* (Urla, 2012) shows that discourses on the Basque language have followed this path. In the chapter "Language loyalism's early roots," she identifies three discursive moments for the language: The first is the Basque dictionary published by Larramendi[1] in the eighteenth century; the second is the literary and folkloric revival of the so-called Basque Renaissance and the creation of the first Basque nationalist political party (Euzko Alderdi Jeltzalea – the Basque Nationalist Party) at the end of the nineteenth century; and the third is linked to the foundation of Eusko Ikaskuntza[2] (the Basque Studies Institute) and Euskaltzaindia[3] (the Basque Language Academy at the beginning of the twentieth century. Although Urla emphasizes these three discursive moments, she also states that discourse on the Basque language dates from much earlier on, long before the emergence of Basque nationalism. By analyzing these three decisive moments, Urla attempts to analyze the relationship between the language and Basque national identity:

1 Manuel de Larramendi (1690–1766).

2 Eusko Ikaskuntza was founded in 1918, and the beginning of the modern period of Basque culture is dated from then.

3 At Eusko Ikaskuntza's first congress (Oñati, 1918), founding the Basque Language Academy was proposed, and this was established in 1918–1919: Euskaltzaindia.

> In juxtaposing these three discursive moments, my aim is to show that within the verifiable long duration of language loyalty, there are notable shifts in the way that loyalists understood the relationship between language and something we might call national identity. Basque has been admired, defended, as well as attacked for a very long time, but not always in the same way or for the same reasons. (Urla, 2012, p. 24)

It is interesting to mention these three discursive moments in order to position today's language discourses. The current discourses on language have not appeared out of nowhere: they are discourses that have changed over time, constructed through the arguments and counter-arguments of each period.

Larramendi published his grammar book *El imposible vencido* (The impossible vanquished) in 1729, and his Spanish-Basque-Latin dictionary in 1745. To place these publications in context, they represent a counter-argument to the view held by eighteenth-century Castilian philologists regarding the dominance of the Spanish language:

> Both of these texts can be seen as early examples of an argument language loyalists would continue to make for another two centuries: namely, that Basque was every bit as grammatically complex, complete, and logical as any other language of high civilization. (Urla, 2012, p. 25)

Urla examines Arturo Campion's and Sabino Arana's[4]

4 Sabino Arana is seen as the "father" of Basque nationalism. He founded the first Basque nationalist party in 1895: Euzko Alderdi Jeltzalea (EAJ; the Basque Nationalist Party).

ideas when studying the Basque Renaissance movement and early Basque nationalism at the end of the nineteenth century. At that time, industrialization and profound demographic changes were taking place in the Basque Country. At the time, primary education was becoming compulsory, and Basque did not play a role in formal education. This was the context in which the Basque Renaissance took place. Arturo Campion was a key figure in the movement, helping to set up the Asociación Euskara de Navarra (Navarrese Basque Association, 1877) and founding its magazine (Revista Euskara, 1878–1883) (Lopez-Antón, 2010). Campion placed the Basque language at the heart of Basque identity:

> His writings and those of his fellow "euskaros" reveal anguish over the decline of Basque, which they saw as both a symptom and a cause of the erosion of a distinctive collective identity. Campión described the Basque language as the most profound aspect of the Basque personality or spirit, "the fundamental, unmistakable, and irreplaceable currency of the Basques." (Iriarte, 2000, p. 324)

Campion criticized the exclusion of the language by the Basque elites, and saw the lack of a university and the non-existence of a unified Basque language as obstacles to adapting Basque to a modern society. Urla describes Campion's language ideology:

> Campión was developing one of the earliest sociolinguistic analyses of the intersection between class, language prestige, and language shift. (Urla, 2012, p. 32)

Campion, however, did not agree with Arana's nationalist party's political vision, which emerged at the same time (Lopez-Antón, 2010). Arana's party—Euzko Alderdi Jeltzalea (the Basque Nationalist Party), founded in 1895—was in line with the Basque cultural imaginary being formed during the Basque Renaissance and was also a pro-independence political movement. As for the Basque language, Basque nationalism understood it to be a symbol of Basque nationality. According to Urla, and as seen by other authors too (Irvine and Gal, 2000), the ideas of nationality that Arana proposed for the Basque Country were those prevalent in Europe at the time:

> Throughout Europe nations were frequently described as races and conceived of as the primordial or natural groupings of humankind analogous to lineages. "Languages" were considered to be the most salient markers of these natural boundaries between peoples. (Urla, 2012, p. 34)

Arana took the same view, arguing that the Basque language was evidence that the Basques were a separate people/race (Urla, 2012).

The third discursive moment that Urla mentions is connected to the creation of Eusko Ikaskuntza and Euskaltzaindia. At the time, she argues, Basque was explicitly conceptualized as an object that required planning. Understanding language as something that can be planned is taken for granted nowadays, but Urla explains that the idea was developed from that point onwards:

> Today, the idea that language is something that can be planned is completely taken for granted. But pausing for a moment to examine the perspectives and proposals of Eusko Ikaskuntza's founders helps bring into focus a time when the idea that language could be planned and should be planned was just beginning to take shape. (Urla, 2012, p. 39)

In Urla's view, this approach was innovative compared to the nostalgic discourse used by the Basque Renaissance. The problems of the Basque language were taken as social problems that could be dealt with:

> The revival of Basque becomes envisioned as a problem treatable through science and planning, like other problems of the city, health, education, or reproduction: that is, as social issues of government that required scientific management and expertise. In the view of this new generation of modernist Basque professionals, protecting the Basque language, culture, and identity required intervention, study, and management, not isolation from "contamination." (Urla, 2012, p. 41)

The first task of the newly founded Euskaltzaindia was to create a unified Basque language. Although there was much debate about this at the time and about how it should be implemented, the process of unification (from the 1960s onwards) established the basis for the language ideology that would prevail from then on, as Urla explains:

> As a process, standardization is at the nexus of the logics of governmentality, modernity, and

> Herderian nationalist imaginary that links one language-one nation. These discourses worked in tandem to render life without Standard Basque unthinkable. (Urla, 2012, p. 45)

So, instead of letting the Basque language take its "natural" path, the academy began to influence its fate:

> In these arguments for scientific study and standardization, we can see clearly how Euskara was being wrenched, at least partially, out of the domain of "nature" (or the divine) where it had resided for so long and incorporated into the domain of "the social." Basque emerges out of these debates not only as a marker of identity or a kind of primordial nationhood, but as a governance social phenomenon to be regulated by experts and requiring new technologies of knowledge measurement, and intervention. (Urla, 2012, p. 47)

Urla examines the final years of the Franco dictatorship, taking into account the changes that happened at that time. The younger generation of the day began to differentiate itself from the Basque Nationalist Party, creating new branches of Basque nationalism, which led to new discourses for understanding the nation and nationality. The link between nation building and the revival of the Basque language became essential in the discourse used by the new generations:

> The revitalization of Basque became for many people of this generation a fundamental form of nation building in which ethnic and non-ethnic

> Basques, native and non-native speakers, could participate. There remains even today, however, a great deal of ambiguity among nationalists about what this concretely means. (Urla, 2012, p. 62)

These generations innovated the discourse about the Basque language, which went from being a symbol of nationality to something that was actually used:

> Language-revival activism at this time did more than treat language as a symbol of the nation; it politicized everyday language use and instantiated a pragmatic view of Basque identity in which being Basque—which for many people meant being Basque nationalist—implied speaking Basque. (Urla, 2012, p. 71)

In her analysis of the discursive path followed in the development of the idea of Basque nationality and the ideology of language, Urla mentions that the new generations of the period used language discourse to develop an ideology of nationalism that is usually termed "civic":

> Language revival is conceptualized as a civic project of sociocultural transformation founded on political beliefs and values in which they sought to engage all of society. It is a form of activism simultaneously cultural and political. (Urla, 2012, p. 68)

At the same time, according to Urla, researchers who have studied Basque nationalism following currents in Western European thought have often understood language as a primordial link with blood and the soul, and have placed the defense of the Basque language and the idea of Basque nationalism within the boundaries of so-called ethnic nationalism. According to Urla, the idea of Basque nationality cannot be placed in the ethnic/civic dichotomy:

> The ethnic, civic, and pragmatic conceptualizations of Basque national identity exist in tension with one another and their disjunctures give rise to the dilemmas and lived contradictions that are the stuff of everyday life in this territory. (Urla, 2012, p. 73)

Whichever way it is conceptualized, there is one key feature in the idea of Basque nationality: the construction of our national identity has never achieved an effective nation-state. This has been the context in which the Basque national identity has developed from its beginnings. The idea of the Basque community existing as a nation on the international scene has suffered its ups and downs, reflecting the varying degrees of institutionalization/deinstitutionalization of the Basques as a national group that has never managed to achieve the degree of institutionalization of a nation-state.

This lack of nation-statehood is of great importance in the study of nationalism. The political arena institutionalized in the form of nation-states is a special institution in that it is considered to be the only organization that can make legitimate use of violence (Ariznabarreta, 2007; Weber, 1975). That is what makes a nation-state unique as an institutional stakeholder and different from other institutions. Human social life is functionally divided into specialized, institutionalized, and interrelated spheres in which each sphere is influenced by the others (Friedland and Alford, 1991). The influence that the state can have on the other spheres of society is different in nature from the influence that other institutions may have on each other. The state is set apart (Krasner, 1993; Lindblom, 1977; Streeck and Schmitter, 1985). This special characteristic gives it the capacity to penetrate every other institutionalized sphere, and the group identity produced and reproduced by the state (the nation) will be reflected in every other sphere of society. The national idea thus penetrates every social sphere of the state.

So, if I were to classify nationalisms, I would not see there to be good and bad nationalisms in a moral sense (Brown, 1999; Calhoun, 2017), but, rather, strong and weak nationalisms depending on the political power they exercise as a group on the international stage.

In this sense, the idea of Basque nationality on the international stage has been, and is, weak, in terms of nationalism compared with other nationalities that have developed state structures. Paradoxically, however, to the extent to which Basque nationalism is known about internationally, it is common for it to be categorized as passionate nationalism, and as Urla points out, many researchers have viewed it as being exclusive and retrograde (Urla, 2012). These readings are closely connected to what Billig has called *banal nationalism*, and which, paradoxically, is an international phenomenon. Following Anderson's idea of nations as imagined communities (Anderson, 1983), in his book *Banal Nationalism* (1995) Billig opened new doors for the study of nationalism, and mentions phenomena that occur as nations consolidate:

> The imagined community ceases to be reproduced by acts of the imagination. In established nations, the imagination becomes inhabited, and, thereby, inhibited. In this sense, the term 'imagined

> community' may be misleading. The community and its place are not so much imagined, but their absence becomes unimaginable. (Billig, 1995, p. 77)

As Billig explains, the nationalism of consolidated nations often goes unnoticed, and, as a result, it is common to say that there are nationalists and non-nationalists in the world. In Spain's case, for example, it is common to use discursive distinctions such as nationalist/constitutionalist when talking about the Basque Country or Catalonia. Basques and Catalans are said to be nationalists, and Spaniards non-nationalists, or constitutionalists. When Billig reflects on nationalism, he mentions that nationalism is often understood as being something uncommon:

> In both popular and academic writing, nationalism is associated with those who struggle to create new states or with extreme right-wing politics. According to customary usage, George Bush is not a nationalist; but separatists in Quebec or Brittany are; so are the leaders of extreme right-wing parties such as the National Front in France; and so, too, are the Serbian guerrillas, killing in the cause of extending the homeland's borders. A book about nationalism is expected to deal with such figures. It should be discussing dangerous and powerful passions, outlining a psychology of extraordinary emotions. (Billig, 1995, p. 5)

When nationalism is understood in this way, the nationalism of Western nation-states is being overlooked. When Billig published *Banal Nationalism*, the way in which these consolidated nationalisms are maintained and reproduced was not usually considered a matter for research; the only subjects worthy of study were "hot" nationalism phenomena—i.e., unusual and passionate phenomena. Billig does not believe that general blindness to the nationalism of consolidated nations, and the fact that they were not labelled as nationalist in political discourse, to be a coincidence:

> Gaps in political language are rarely innocent. The case of 'nationalism' is no exception. By being semantically restricted to small sizes and exotic colours, 'nationalism' becomes identified as a problem: it occurs 'there' on the periphery, not 'here' in the centre. (Billig, 1995, p. 6)

To study the phenomenon of nationalism in a general way, Billig used the term *banal nationalism*:

> The term *banal nationalism* is introduced to cover the ideological habits which enable the established nations of the West to be reproduced. It is argued that these habits are not removed from everyday life, as some observers have assumed. Daily, the nation is indicated, or 'flagged,' in the lives of its citizenry. Nationalism, far from being an intermittent mood in established nations, is the endemic condition. (Billig, 1995, p. 6)

In this book, which has had a major impact on the study of nationalism, Billig focuses on the discursive actions used by consolidated nation-states to reproduce the nation in a banal way, using less obvious, everyday ways of praising the nation:

> "National identity" is a short-hand for a whole series of familiar assumptions about nationhood, the world and "our" place in that world. . . . These assumptions have to be flagged discursively. And for that, banal words, jingling in the ears of citizens, or passing before their eyes, are required. (Billig, 1995, p. 93)

As Urla points out, the Basque language revival movement in the twentieth century was powerfully influenced by both Basque and Spanish nationalist ideology. I could also point out the influence of French nationalist ideology here. But, as I have stated before, because the idea of Basque nationalism has not been institutionalized as a consolidated nation-state, its reproduction possesses certain peculiarities compared with the reproduction of the consolidated Spanish and French nationalisms.

Australian actor Jacob Elordi was at the center of a controversy that gives us a glimpse of the lack of consolidation of the Basque national identity. Journalists from various media outlets reported on the commotion Elordi had created on social media (*Berria*, August 3, 2020; *El Diario Vasco*, August 8, 2020) by posting a video of himself correcting his Wikipedia profile. The headline was that the actor had denied his Spanish ancestry. Apparently, Elordi's grandfather was Basque and would have "strangled him" if his grandson had said he was Spanish. The actor explains in the video that his ancestors came from the Basque Country, adding that it is a country between France and Spain. So the actor replaces the word "Spanish" with "Basque" in the Wikipedia entry and posts a video of himself doing so, angering Spanish nationalists so much that they removed his correction from Wikipedia. Elordi has reedited the entry several times. The extensive coverage of the story in the Basque media is a further reflection of the lack of consolidation of Basque nationalism. If it were a consolidated nation, the correction of such a mistake in Wikipedia would receive little media attention—it would be just a correction of an unintentional mistake. The actor himself would probably not have cared so much if the "inaccuracy" had involved two consolidated nations, for example "Italian" instead of "Spanish." It would not have been an ideological mistake and would likely not have aroused such interest. The lack of consolidation of Basque national identity, however, makes the news item important and reveals the Basque nationality's lack of banality. When it comes to reporting, too, it is also interesting to examine the rhetoric used by journalists from a national perspective. From a Basque nationalistic point of view, the way the actor is described underlines his youth and prosperous professional career, and lends credibility to his words (e.g., *Berria, Naiz*). From a Spanish nationalistic perspective, however, the language used to undermine the image of the actor is noteworthy. For example, in the newspaper *ABC*, the story begins: "He may well be one of the least loved characters in the first season of *Euphoria*." A few lines later, the journalist adds: ". . . with his statements about his origins, he has certainly earned a few more haters than he already had because of his temper." The headline used by the Spanish newspaper is also significant: "Jacob Elordi, the actor from *Euphoria* who denies his Spanish ancestry: 'I am descended from Basques.' " When the word *deny* is used, it is suggested that the Spanish identity of the actor's ancestors is unquestionable, depriving the actor's words of credibility (*ABC*, August 4, 2020). By using this completely anecdotal news item as an example, my aim is to emphasize that, as the Basque nation is an unconsolidated nation, its reproduction does not take place in the same way as that of consolidated nations. In an unconsolidated nation, what is ordinary for a consolidated nation becomes extraordinary; conversely, what is extraordinary for a consolidated nation becomes ordinary.

In a consolidated nation the national language, too, is inadvertently reproduced: naturally, normally, in a banal way. Basque, on the other hand, is not reproduced naturally or normally. Singer Ruper Ordorika talked about how difficult it is to be Basque in the song *Zaindu maite duzu hori* (Mind what you love, from the 2003 album *Kantuok jartzen ditut*). The lyrics were written by Ordorika in a specific context. At the time he wrote the song, the only newspaper written in Basque (*Euskaldunon Egunkaria*—"The Basques' Newspaper") had been closed down by order of the Spanish National Court.

The lack of consolidation of the Basque language and of Basque national identity results in—when it comes to reproducing them—a high level of awareness of these identities. Just as many members of consolidated nation-states do not consider themselves nationalists, and many examples of nationalistic behavior go unnoticed, most Basque nationalists are well aware of the fact that they are nationalists. To reproduce national identity, one must constantly, on a daily basis, overcome the obstacles posed by the lack of banality (and the banality of other national identities), and achieving this unconsciously is not an easy thing to do. So Basque national identity is characterized by a high degree of self-awareness.

5. The discursive complexity of Basque nationalism

Daddy says there was a king who rained for forty years.
F. Gwynne. *The King Who Rained.*

When I say that the way Basque nationalism is reproduced is different from the way that Spanish, French, or any other consolidated nationalism is reproduced, I do not acknowledge that a dichotomy exists between banal and hot nationalism. I do not believe that Spanish and French nationalisms are reproduced in a banal way while Basque nationalism is reproduced in a hot way. Starting with Michael Billig's innovative perspective on nationality, a wealth of work has been carried out on the subject, and the study of numerous specific cases has revealed many inherent nuances (Skey and Antonsich, 2017). In fact, several authors have focused on hot and banal forms of nationalism and how they are interrelated (Hutchinson, 2006; Jones and Merriman, 2009).

Skey (2009), for example, says that there are varying degrees between "hot" and "cold" nationalism, and that the use of the terms "hot" and "cold" nationalism is not accurate. According to Skey, by understanding the reproduction of a nation as a process, it is more useful to use the concepts of "heating" and "cooling" nationalist temperatures. He argues that these concepts emphasize the degrees between the extremes. Billig agrees with this:

> Hopefully, such phrases will encourage investigators to point to the ways that actors might be heating up or cooling down moments of nationalism. (Billig, 2017, p. 314)

According to Billig, the misunderstandings that the use of the terms "hot" and "cold" nationalism can lead to do not end there, and he states the importance of clarifying that at any one moment in the history of nationalism there is no single temperature, emphasizing thus the complexity of the subject:

> It is a mistake – and a mistake to be found in Banal Nationalism – to suppose that every moment in the history of nationalism can be summarized by a single temperature. The heating and cooling of nationalism can occur at the same time in the same place. (Billig, 2017, p. 314)

All these researchers give an idea of the complexities involved when researching Basque nationalism. When approaching the subject, there are many factors that need to be taken into account. For one thing, it is important to avoid the misinterpretations that hot/banal distinctions can lead to. For another, there are two crucial, interconnected points that must not be forgotten, and which I will discuss here in further detail. The first of these is that the Basque nation is produced "within" the other two nations; and the second point is that differences in levels of self-awareness exist between nations being produced and consolidated nations which are being reproduced.

The first point is connected to the study of the complexities involved in national (re)production when the nation in question is located "within" another nation.

In a study conducted by Rosie and colleagues in the UK, articles in various newspapers were examined, focusing on the "national framework" used. Their study revealed the complexity of the topic (Rosie, MacInnes, Petersoo, Condor & Kennedy, 2004). In contexts where the idea of more than one nation "overlaps," such as in the Basque Country, the complexity these researchers encountered is reflected by the media.

I will begin by recalling an episode that took place several years ago and which demonstrates the complexity of how nations are reproduced in the media. There was a great deal of controversy about the weather map on Basque public television (EiTB) in 2009 when Patxi Lopez, a member of the Socialist Party of the Basque Country, PSE (a branch of the Spanish Socialist Party, PSOE), was nominated president of the Basque Government. At the time, the Basque left-wing party had been banned. Several Spanish newspapers, including *El País*, described Lopez as the first "non-nationalist" president in history, implying that all presidents before him had been "nationalists" (*El País*, May 5, 2009). *El País,* which, as its name clearly indicates, banally reproduces consolidated Spanish nationality, nevertheless attributed the nationalist category to Basque nationalists in their headline. As soon as Patxi Lopez became president of the Basque Government, several changes were made; among them, the weather map on Basque public television was changed. Up until then, the map had shown all seven provinces of the Basque Country, in keeping with the Basque nationalist imagery of seven provinces forming one unit. During Lopez's legislature, the image of the Basque Country's seven provinces was removed and replaced with the one showing only some of the Basque provinces located within Spain; however, when the Basque Nationalist Party (EAJ-PNV) returned to the presidency in 2013, the weather map of the seven provinces (albeit with clear administrative demarcation lines) was restored once again to Basque television screens.

This particular example of media coverage might lead one to think that when Basque nationalists are in power in the Basque Government, the production and reproduction of Basque nationalism takes place in different spheres, including publicly-owned media. On closer examination, however, while the EiTB weather map does show the seven provinces—and in this sense the imagery of Basque nationalism is being reproduced—it cannot be concluded that the discourse used on public media is generally favorable to the production of Basque nationalism. In unconsolidated nations, the way nationalist discourse is reproduced is not that simple. A mixture of ambiguous, confusing discourse, and discourses that are useful for the reproduction of different nations, may appear on the same media. The discourse of some EiTB programs reflects the national image of the seven provinces of the Basque Country. One example is *Herri Txiki, Infernu Haundi*, a show in which the presenters travel throughout the seven provinces of the Basque Country, interviewing the local people, recording their stories, and learning about their life and work. This program shows the Basque Country as a country made up of seven provinces. Another similar example is the broadcast of the most important Basque Country bertsolaritza (improvised poetry) championship. Here the participants and audience members hail from all seven provinces, and rounds of the competition are held in each province. However, on the same channel's news programs, it is not uncommon to hear the "National High Court" being mentioned, with no explicit reference to the fact that the court in question is the Spanish national court. This is a clear example of banal reproduction of the Spanish nation. Even when it comes to classifying news, a Spanish event may be given priority, such as, for example, a case of gender violence. While cases of gender-based violence in Germany or Serbia are not reported, the Spanish national image is reproduced in a banal way when such news items from Spain are concerned. What I mean by these examples is that the production and reproduction of different nations in the Basque Country is not entirely differentiated in the media, in institutions, or in ordinary everyday conversation.

One might think that the allegedly moderate stance of the Basque Nationalist Party (EAJ-PNV) is responsible for the vague and confusing reproduction of nationality in the discourse of the Basque public broadcaster. However, this confusion also persists in the so-called "more radical" left-wing nationalist media. For example, when reporting on the coronavirus epidemic, the newspaper *GARA* presented data for the Peninsular Basque Country (Hegoalde) (*GARA*, August 8, 2020). By using the concept of "Hegoalde" it infers that "Iparralde" (Continental Basque Country) also exists, although no data about the latter is provided. In this way, a picture of a seven-province Basque Country is reproduced. Although the aim is to provide news about the seven-province Basque Country, no national statistics institute exists for this territory—unlike in consolidated nation-states—so the newspaper is unable to offer comprehensive data all at once and has to resort to publishing such items in installments.

And when it comes to classifying the news, some newspapers include "Basque Country" and "World" sections while other newspapers do not have specific "Basque Country" sections. Including dedicated sections transmits the message that the Basque Country is a nation in the world of nations. On *GARA*'s *Naiz* digital platform, for example, the "World" section featured a news story about the king of Spain (August 10, 2020). Being classified as world news, readers see that he is not thought of as the king of the nation, and thus it could be considered as a case of Basque national reproduction. However, upon closer examination, it is clear that such a simple interpretation of the headline falls short. The headline reads: "Proceedings against representatives of BNG, Adelante Andalucía and ERC for 'insults to the Crown.' " It is assumed that the reader knows what the initials stand for, and which crown is being referred to. If a newspaper reports on a foreign event in a different nation with a different national point of view, it would state clearly in the headline which nation it is talking about. It cannot assume that readers of the "World" section know which country it is referring to. When the initials of foreign political parties or groups are used, an explanation is usually given. In this particular news item, the words "Parliament" and "National Court Prosecution Service" are also mentioned with no extra information given. This is an example of how a news item placed in the "World" section, which could have potentially been a reproduction of Basque nationalism, also contained a banal reproduction of Spanish nationalism in the background.

Several more news items about the king of Spain appeared in August 2020 in *GARA* publications. On August 5, for example, the headline on the front page of the newspaper read: "Sanchez remains silent about the ex-king while praising '78" (*GARA*, August 5, 2020). This headline would not be readily understood outside the Spanish national context. There are several details in the headline that would resonate within a Spanish national context (apart from the significance of finding it on the front page). "Sanchez" needs no explanation.

The reader knows who we are talking about. Nor does "ex-king." And when " '78" is referred to, it is assumed that the reader knows that it is 1978. The " '78 regime" is so called because the current Spanish political regime was founded in 1978 when King Juan Carlos Bourbon of Spain became king on the request of dictator Francisco Franco. The headline criticizes the "regime of '78" because, although it advanced the aim of "democracy," "the Franco dictatorship achieved impunity," and King Juan Carlos personified the restoration of the Bourbon monarchy. This headline assumes that the reader is aware of these details and therefore understands it. In the same way, a few days later, in the newspaper's comic strip section, cartoonist Tasio used the word "monarchy" (*GARA*, August 9, 2020). If readers are to understand the humor intended by this, they need to be aware of the Spanish national context.

Another example of how the different nations are reproduced simultaneously can be found in Basque cinema and TV listings. The newspaper *GARA* publishes the cinema programs for all seven provinces of the Basque Country and includes TV schedules for the Basque, Spanish, and French television channels. It also publishes a weather map of the seven territories.

As a final example, on August 2, 2020, *GARA* published a news item about the future of the economy in its "Current Affairs" section. Entitled "Crisis and Recovery Plans," it was about the economic crisis caused by the coronavirus pandemic. Under the headline, it read: "Frightened by the future economy, Basque employers have taken the initiative to propose a nationwide pact." When Basque employers are mentioned in that sentence, it becomes clear that they are referring to the Confebask association. According to its website, Confebask is the

"Basque Employers' Confederation," a confederation that defends the general interests of "Basque" businessmen and women and companies, and is the legal representative of companies and employers in their dealings with the public administration, trade unions, etc. They do all this "in Euskadi," operating in the provinces of Gipuzkoa, Bizkaia, and Araba. They also claim to be members of the Spanish Confederation of Employers. But if the *GARA* readers are not aware of this beforehand, they might naturally associate the words "Basque employers" with all seven provinces in the Basque Country, and when a "nationwide pact" is mentioned, they could assume it refers to the seven-province Basque Country. The country is not specified at any stage in the article. When Confebask makes statements such as "from the Basque Country," they may be thinking of companies from Gipuzkoa, Bizkaia, and Araba. Further on, when it says, "seen from the Basque Country, a small country," it is not very clear whether they are talking about seven provinces or three. And in sentences such as "our country is not exactly a paradise where nothing is needed," which country exactly are they referring to when they say "our country"?

What we see with these examples is that, when it comes to unconsolidated nations, many nuances must be taken into account when studying the reproduction of nationalist ideology, and this has been examined in several other contexts as well (Law, 2001). The separation line between the reproduction of the Spanish/French nation and the reproduction of the Basque nation is not easy to draw . An examination of media reports gives us an idea of the confusion of words used in the Basque Country when talking about nationality. Concepts that are readily understood in consolidated nations cannot be taken for granted in unconsolidated nation states.

For instance, the style book of the newspaper *Berria* is available on its website. The book starts by explaining the origin of the newspaper, stating that Euskarazko Komunikabide Taldea (EKT – Basque Language Media Group) was founded in 2003 with the aim of creating and promoting Basque language media following the closure of *Euskaldunon Egunkaria*. They state that the first mission of EKT was to open a new national newspaper in Basque. Thus, *Berria* was founded within this context, and so it might be thought of as a tool for producing the idea of Basque nationality. The point is that when nationality is produced/reproduced in discourse, the term "nation" can have multiple interpretations or meanings (MacInnes, Rosie, Petersoo, Condor & Kennedy, 2007). When the style book mentions, for example, that the newspaper aimed to take into account all sensibilities within the Basque community, the meaning of the word "Basque" does not appear to be connected with the imagery of the Basque nation-state but, rather, with all political points of view. Thus, the term might seem to be used for cultural purposes, or to refer to a geographical territory. However, in the "territory and community" section of the style book, it says that *Berria*'s nation is the Basque Country and specifies that this means the seven-province Basque Country. It also clarifies that the word "Euskadi" is not used unless it appears in the proper names of institutions or groups of public administration organizations within the BAC (Basque Autonomous Community), nor is it ever used as a geographical reference, thus implicitly rejecting the "official" three-province Euskadi. Regarding the names of institutions, magazines, and associations, they use the names used by the organizations themselves, even though they know, for example, that the "University of the Basque Country" is, in fact, the University of the

Basque Autonomous Community. It defines how they use the word "Basque," the concept of a Basque citizen, the concept of a Basque speaker, and other terms. What the style book shows us is that instructions are needed so that the reader can understand the terminology correctly because some words have many different uses. In other words, these terms and concepts are used rhetorically with different meanings in the Basque Country.

With regard to the previously mentioned second point, and in reference to a study on Serbia (Spasić, 2017), Billig mentions the differences between the process of creating a nation-state and the reproduction of consolidated nations:

> Spasić is correct to suggest that the processes of reproducing a nation state differ from those involved in producing or creating the nation state in the first place. . . . The original formation of most nation states, which have become established over time, was violent and backed by imaginative and highly conscious declarations about the nature of the state, its people and its claimed territory. . . . When *Banal Nationalism* was originally written, Serbia was in the process of being produced, rather than being reproduced. If there is a difference between the first edition *Banal Nationalism* and the preface for the Serbian edition, it is that Serbian history has moved on. From being a nation, which was in the violent process of being produced, Serbia by 2009 was becoming a nation state which will be banally reproduced. (Billig, 2017, p. 311)

The idea of a Basque nation, as mentioned above, has been an idea in production from its inception until today, but it has not been consolidated as a nation-state, and, therefore, the ideas have not reached the banal reproduction typical of consolidated nation-states. Therefore, the idea of Basque nationalism has been (and is being) produced with a high level of self-awareness and a corresponding level of self-criticism. In her book *Reclaiming Basque*, Jaqueline Urla mentions criticisms of counter-hegemonic movements:

> Movements for racial, sexual, and gender equality, for example, are critiqued for reproducing essentialist notions of identity; ecology movements are revealed to uphold conservative notions of nature. This type of criticism has also been levelled at minority language movements: in working to ensure greater respect and status for their language, activists' images, beliefs, and goals reproduce some of the dominant ways that nation-states conceptualize and treat languages: for example, the notion of languages as bounded, discrete objects, the belief in the necessity of internal uniformity; the erection of norms of good and bad use; and a presumed unambiguous link between nation and language. (Urla, 2012, p. 16)

In this sense, Basque nationalism, along with many other sub-state nationalisms, produces/reproduces a nationalist ideology that is international and global, as Billig puts it (Billig, 2017, p. 311). It is taken for granted that the world is made up of nations, and, using the idea of Basque nationality, it is argued that the Basque nation is one of them. Through defense of the nation, the international hegemonic idea of a world made up of natural nations is reproduced. The fact is that many of the agents involved in the production of the unconsolidated Basque nation are aware of these criticisms. The high degree of awareness of nationalism implies this; due to the widespread bad reputation of nationalism, people's self-awareness of being nationalists creates a certain discomfort. Therefore, debates that do not arise in many consolidated nations do arise within the context of Basque nationalism. In this sense, it is important to understand, for example, the debate on the social/national dichotomy that intensified from the 1960s onwards. It has been, and still is, an ideological dilemma within Basque nationalism (Billig, Condor, Edwards, Gane, Middleton & Radley, 1988). Whether the social and national problem can be understood separately (and which of the two should be given priority), or whether they are inseparable from each other, is at the heart of the debate. These debates include, for example, that which led to the split within the armed group Euskadi ta askatasuna (ETA) (Giacopuzzi, 1997; Jauregui, 1981; Urla, 2012). When Billig and Marinho examine the rhetoric of the commemoration of the 1974 revolution in Portugal in the book "The politics and rhetoric of commemoration" (Billig and Marinho, 2017), they show that different ideological dilemmas arise in consolidated nation-states. Billig himself, referring to the mentioned book, says:

> Sometimes, in these celebrations, speakers from the right will dispute with those from the left about the term 'the people' (o povo). Both, however, will accept the nationalist meaning of the term: in the context of the celebration, 'the people' refers to the people of Portugal. (Billig, 2017, p. 318)

Many ideological dilemmas that do not occur in consolidated nation-states do arise in unconsolidated nations, to the point of questioning or denying the very existence of the nation. This does not mean that such dilemmas cannot arise within consolidated nations. To the extent that nations are as dynamic and rhetorical as any institution, there is always the potential for such debate and controversy (Billig, 1987). But the level of institutionalization conditions the questioning of the various "truths" that are taken to be knowledge, and, as a result, nation-states that are not effectively institutionalized constantly question their own nation (and the concept of the state itself).

The very degree of the self-awareness of unconsolidated nationalisms can lead to changes in the way the nation is built. This, too, helps to explain the words of researcher Sanjay Jeram, as reported by Larraitz Ariznabarreta in her book *Notes on Basque Culture*:

> The political elite of non-state nationalist movements is becoming more civic and progressive than their state contemporaries in order to establish their legitimacy on the international stage. (Ariznabarreta, 2019, p. 118)

As a result, when other authors have carried out research on the attitude of sub-state nations to immigration (Adam, 2013; Barker, 2010; Hepburn, 2009), contrary to what many have argued (Kymlicka, 2001), it transpired that several sub-state nations chose multiculturalism over assimilation. In the Basque Country, the policies of the Basque Government and the vision of EAJ have been studied (Jeram and Adam, 2015; Jeram, 2016) and reveal that the decision to choose multiculturalism is related to past readings of Basque nationalism:

> Narratives of cultural oppression have been essential for nationalist mobilization in the Basque Country and Flanders. In turn, the choice of multiculturalism over assimilation by sub-state elites made sense because it fits with their understanding of the nation as an oppressed group. (Jeram & Adam, 2015, p.241)

Being an unconsolidated nation-state means that justification has to be given for any step related to the production of Basque nationality. An example of this might be the Ikastola movement. Every nation-state organizes its mass education system to integrate new generations into the ideological we-ness created by the state (Zabaleta-Imaz, 2000). In the Basque Country, in the absence of effective state structures, a network of schools based on Basque national we-ness was created under clandestine circumstances. This movement was called the Ikastola movement, and Basque schools were called Ikastolas (Erize, 2003; Iza, 2010). Outside Spanish legality, and sometimes in a semi-legal way, the transmission of the national we-ness and the Basque language was the central aim of these schools. Since the founding of the autonomous communities in Spain, the question of how to integrate Basque Ikastolas into the broader general education system has been an important subject of debate, the result of which is that these Basque schools currently belong to this larger system. Some of the Ikastolas joined the Spanish public education system, while others were turned into semi-private schools eligible for public grants. The desire to rid themselves of the derogatory nationalist label they had been given is probably what led them to constantly proclaim their open, diverse nature.

Similarly, other Basque nation-related initiatives have constantly had to prove their openness and show that diversity can be a trademark of the unconsolidated construction of the Basque nation (Jeram, 2013).

As mentioned in the previous chapter, ideologies about language are closely linked to ideologies about the nation. The points I have touched on in this chapter give an idea of the discursive complexity that is also encountered when discussing the Basque language. The term "Basque nation" can be used to refer to a cultural community in the seven provinces, but it can also be used to refer to the autonomous community in Spain called "Euskadi" which is made up of three provinces; it can designate a nation with aspirations of becoming a state of seven provinces or can refer to a people that wants to recover its own state. Similarly, Basque can also be the national language of the Basques, or it can be thought of as something else. So, who are the Basques? What is the Basque nation? Is it an ethnic language? Joxe Manuel Odriozola wanted to answer these questions in his book *Nora goaz euskalduntasun honekin?* (Where are we going with this Basqueness? 2017). He wrote his reflection on the Basque language in an attempt to shed light on the controversies that surround the languages of unconsolidated nations.

I believe that the category "Basque nationalism" is problematic. Since the ideology of the Basque nation first emerged years ago, a multitude of ideas about the Basque nation have been created, recreated, abandoned, and overshadowed. I believe many studies to be biased inasmuch as they do not question the true status of organizations or movements that define themselves as "Basque nationalists." From a discursive point of view, "conceptual diversity" about Basque nationalism can also be found in reference to the Basque language, because as

Urla pointed out in her study, discourses on language and nation are intertwined. From the discursive reproduction of the nation, I can say that the "Basque nation" is "all of that" mentioned before, and at the same time "nothing at all." The "Basque nation" is made up of unconsolidated ideological "confusion." Basque, too, is everything and nothing.

6. The people Iof the Basque language?

All peoples have the right to self-determination; by virtue of that right they freely determine their political status and freely pursue their economic, social and cultural development. Universal Declaration of Human Rights.
United Nations. December 14, 1960.

In the social sciences, the debate between the perspectives of "individualism" vs. "collectivism" (sometimes called "holism") has a long history (Soares, 2018). As with most concepts, defining individualism is not straightforward (Lukes, 1971). In order to somehow simplify the use I am going to make of it throughout the chapter, and following Soares, I consider individualism to be an attitude rather than a theory:

> [Individualism] is probably best described as a tendency or an attitude, the tendency or the attitude of centering on the idea that the individual human being is a maker of the world he/she inhabits. (Soares, 2018, p. 16)

Unlike in the collectivist point of view, from the individualist perspective, society is seen as a mere collection of individuals, not something over and above them. From a collectivist point of view, however, society is more than just a set of autonomous individuals. Societies have an order and a structure that make them more than just groups of independently acting individuals. In the philosophy of Western society, although the individualist view has become very important since the Enlightenment, it has also encountered challenges from the counter-arguments of the collectivist view (Soares, 2018).

In the book *Ideological Dilemmas* (Billig et al, 1988), the authors make the point that there are dilemmas within ideologies. Ideologies do not form a coherent corpus, but, rather, a set of controversial ideas. In the chapter *Dilemmas of ideology*, the ideological dilemmas of Enlightenment individualism are examined. The values of the liberty, equality, and fraternity of the French Revolution are taken as examples. The authors highlight the controversy over values and ideas based on individual freedom and equality:

> If liberty were to be individual freedom, then it was necessary to establish why the individual should show loyalty to the state and social responsibility to fellow individuals. Liberty would result in anarchy lest some form of authority could be established. Nor should it be forgotten that the modern capitalist era may have freed individuals from feudal restrictions, but it has also seen the emergence of the state in its most powerful form. (Billig et al, 1988, p. 36)

They highlight the controversy over the ideas in the Enlightenment:

> The rationality of the Enlightenment *philosophes* was a universal rationality, which knew no national boundaries. . . . Yet the world of individualism has not been a world which has seen the crumbling of nationality. Far from it; the governmental states, which have grown so powerful in the past

> two hundred years, have been national states demanding national allegiance from their freely individual and politically equal members. (Billig et al, 1988, p. 36)

The position that researchers take as a starting point for the study of social phenomena, leaning their arguments towards one side or the other of the controversy, can completely condition the conclusions they draw about any given phenomenon. Rhetoric shows us this; a position and its opposite can be defended, and both can be properly argued positions (Billig, 1987). Through different arguments and discourses, we construct the social reality we are studying in one way or another. Through our words and other actions, we can achieve results of one kind or another on the same subject.

Researchers David and Derthick examined the phenomenon of internalized oppression in a book of the same name: *Internalized Oppression. The Psychology of Marginalized Groups* (David, 2014). Using an interesting example, they show how the choice of approach when studying a given phenomenon can impact the results. Using the subject of skin whitening products, they cite the number of users worldwide and explain how the World Health Organization (WHO) considers the phenomenon to be a global health problem because of the possible side effects of the products. The authors criticize the approach taken by the WHO when studying the problem. According to the WHO, skin whitening products, especially those that contain a large amount of mercury, can lead to serious skin and kidney problems, among other things. As a result, the organization called for policy changes to control the amount of mercury in these products. In David and Derthick's view, however, reducing the problem to a "mercury problem" is problematic: "This limited conceptualization conceals the fact that an important contributor to the problem is oppression and internalized oppression, phenomena women, men, and children throughout the world experience" (David and Derthick, 2014, p. 1). Both approaches can be argued rhetorically and will lead to different conclusions and point to different courses of action to remedy the problem. The example is not given in order to discuss the "truth" of one position or another. The point is that when analyzing a social problem, the consequences will be different depending on the starting point, and people's thinking and actions will also be different depending on the framework they use to position the topic. It is precisely in this example that the ideological dilemma I refer to throughout this chapter is revealed: the ideological dilemma of individualism-holism. When it comes to setting the framework, one approach focuses on individuals, while the other focuses on social structures:

> By keeping oppression out of the conversation, it makes it appear as though the problem and the blame belong completely to the individuals (e.g., they are not satisfied with self, and they are consuming harmful chemicals). Alternatively, if we frame the problem as oppression, then we necessarily must look for factors outside the individual – historical and contemporary sociopolitical factors – which may influence the use of such products. (David & Derthick, 2014, p. 1)

Feminist researcher Ann E. Cudd, in her book *Analyzing Oppression*, expresses her position on the individualism-collectivism controversy (Cudd, 2006). Her theory of the phenomenon of oppression is based on social groups and social institutions. If, from the point of view of individualists, social groups are merely sets of individuals, social theories should not be based on social groups. Cudd reflects on the concept of social groups to justify her position. Researchers, explicitly or not, examine social phenomena from a certain position, and social structures, along with the concept of the social groups related to them, are controversial concepts, as Perelman and Olbrechts-Tyteca have pointed out:

> In short, the concept of group is an argumentative element of a highly controversial and unstable nature, but of the utmost importance. (Perelman & Olbrechts-Tyteca, 1969, p. 323)

After mentioning the different perspectives that can exist among researchers on the concept of social groups, Cudd talks about voluntary and non-voluntary social groups, and specifies details about the two types of groups. She argues that we are participants in different social groups. We join some of these groups voluntarily, while, in others, our membership is not chosen individually (Cudd, 2006). Among researchers who consider social groups to be real, many different positions can be found. Cudd focuses on a fundamental disagreement among these researchers, classifying the individualism-collectivism debate into two main perspectives: the intentionalist and the structuralist. While these views are often considered incompatible, Cudd adopts a compatibilist approach:

> I shall be arguing here for a compatibilist position, holding that while all action is intentionally guided, many of the constraints within which we

> act are socially determined and beyond the control of the currently acting individual; to put a slogan on it, intentions dynamically interact within social structures. (Cudd, 2006, p. 36)

From Cudd's perspective here, the intentionality of individuals is fundamental when it comes to interpreting actions, but at the same time she also takes on the structuralists' point of view, arguing that social structures cannot be reduced to individual actions alone (Cudd, 2006).

Within the discipline of social psychology, renowned researchers such as Tajfel (primarily known for his theory of Social Identity), Moscovici, and many others have encountered and addressed the individual-society dilemma. In the first part of the book *The Context of Social Psychology,* edited by Israel and Tajfel (Israel and Tajfel, 1972), for example, the two chapters written by Moscovici and Tajfel reflect the authors' concerns. In the introduction to the book, Tajfel mentions the reciprocal influence of humans and society. Referring to the mentioned two chapters in the first part of the book, his and Moscovici´s, he states:

They present an argument for the transformation of what is being done at present into a genuinely social psychology which would have as its basis the idea that Man and society have a reciprocal effect upon the mode of existence and behaviour of each other; thus, they call for the rejection of concepts implying a one-way causation, whatever direction the causation is presumed to take. (Tajfel, 1972, p. 5)

In Billig's prolific work, too, there is continual reflection on the reciprocal influence between the individual and society. Like Tajfel, he does not accept one-way causation. In the aforementioned and well-known book *Ideological Dilemmas*, Billig and his colleagues make their point clear:

In stressing the dilemmatic aspects of ideology, we hope to oppose the implications of both cognitive and ideological theory, which ignore the social nature of thinking. In contrast to the cognitive psychologists, we stress the ideological nature of thought; in contrast to theorists of ideology, we stress the thoughtful nature of ideology. (Billig et al, 1988, p. 2)

Views that consider human thought in isolation have been criticized, as have those that have seen humans as slaves by emphasizing social structures. Here again, Billig is critical of both positions in which the "disappearing of society" and the "disappearing of the individual" occur. The latter position offers an obedient, passive view of man, which Billig does not accept, but in the former, the individual takes center stage, and power relations are not taken into account:

> The inequalities of power, and the domination of one class over another, have little place in this sort of social psychological investigation. (Billig, 1991, p. 9)

According to Cudd there are voluntary and non-voluntary groups, and there is a continuum between the two poles. She takes an externalist approach to the study of social groups. In this way, the constraints that people experience from the outside are emphasized:

> What makes a person a member of a social group is not determined by any internal states of that person, but rather by objective facts about the world, including how others perceive and behave toward that person. (Cudd, 2006, p. 36)

According to this externalist view, not all groups are voluntary, and that being so, externally imposed constraints are necessary, and can be sufficient, for social group membership (Cudd, 2006, p. 37). This view is related to what Perelman and Olbrechts-Tyteca say:

> Although the reality of a group may depend on the attitude of its members, it depends as much or even more on the attitude of outsiders. These like to think that a social group exists, whenever they themselves behave differently toward the members of the group. (Perelman & Olbrechts-Tyteca, 1969, p. 323)

When external social constraints are mentioned, Cudd is referring to institutionally structured constraints, and these, ultimately, define social groups in terms of social institutions:

> Social groups are collections of individuals who face common constraints that are structured by social institutions. (Cudd, 2006, p. 51)

In the Basque Country, the study of individualism and collectivism is of particular importance in the analysis of thought about nation and language. According to the United Nations article quoted at the beginning of this chapter, all peoples have the right to self-determination.

That being the case, the controversy in politics is about what a nation is, and what it is not. A community that wants to self-determine will argue that it is a nation, and will justify this rhetorically, criticizing arguments to the contrary.

Political thinker Joseba Ariznabarreta published his book *Pueblo y Poder. Cuadernos para la reconstrucción de la razón* (People and Power. Notes towards the reconstruction of reasoning) more than a decade ago (Ariznabarreta, 2007). In the book, the first chapter reflects on the concept of the People, and the individual-society ideological dilemma reappears. The author cites the ideas of authors who favor an individualistic approach to the study of politics in order to rhetorically disagree with their arguments, and he argues that in social sciences, human beings must be analyzed as belonging to "groups," which are not aggregates of individuals. Moving away from the essentialist view of defining a people, he states:

> The difficulty arises from the attempt to search for characteristics whose common presence would allow them to become reality in hindsight, as if the existence of a nation could be confused with a required set (by whom?) of predicates. (Ariznabarreta, 2007, p. 34)

He argues that the basic factor in defining the group is power, and because of the exercise of this power, groups do or do not exist. A "people" arises when a group exercises its power. When a people ceases to exercise power, it ceases to exist. In a similar vein, Ann E. Cudd refers to the institutionalized social constraints that we come across in reality. The arguments of both authors fall within the individualism-collectivism ideological dilemma which crops up repeatedly in social sciences. Cudd takes an externalist view in response to the individualistic views that sometimes emerge within feminism, arguing that a social group of women exists: "My account assumes that in the world there are constraints that apply to all women, others to all men, others to all African Americans, and so forth" (Cudd, 2006, p. 47).

Joseba Ariznabarreta, in turn, argues in favor of the existence of the people, rejecting the idea of a set of autonomous individuals. In his book, the author adopts his stance on the matter while also responding rhetorically to the individualistic view that was gaining momentum in wider Basque society at the time of the book's publication. Ariznabarreta emphasizes the group, but his view should not be oversimplified or confused with the unidirectional views mentioned by Tajfel. His counter-arguments against this individualist view echo the point Billig makes here in response to the criticism he received on his book *Banal Nationalism*:

> As can often happen, social scientists, who aim to draw attention to phenomena that have previously been overlooked, can emphasize their case rhetorically by presenting clear exemplars. (Billig, 2017, p. 313)

Over the last two decades, an individualistic approach has become prevalent in public discourse in the Basque Country. In 2001, a proposal was presented for a new political status for the Basque Autonomous Community, known as the "Ibarretxe Plan" (in reference to Juan Jose Ibarretxe, the president of the BAC government at that time). Although it was rejected as soon as it reached

Madrid, the ideas in the plan filtered down into Basque society. The "right to decide" was mentioned in the proposal. The concept of the "right to decide," which had prevailed over the "right to self-determination," reinforced an individualistic approach to focusing on the political problem of the Basque Country. From this perspective, the emphasis was placed on the individual instead of on the nation. By moving away from the structural change required by the philosophical view of an oppressed people, the emphasis was placed on the will of individuals rather than on structural barriers or advantages. In this way, a democratic framework was represented in which people could express their opinions about the future of the Basque Country freely and without interference. This individualistic approach can be observed in Basque politics and in the media when the use of specific words such as "society" and "people" is examined (Billig, 1995). Concepts such as the "Basque people" or "Basque nation" are replaced with the word "society." Ariznabarreta's work must be understood as a counter-argument to this individual-empowering ideology. His view is that emphasizing the "people" brings with it the need to place the opinions of individuals in context.

This ideological dilemma is also reflected in the area of the Basque language. As mentioned in the third chapter, positive individual attitudes and motivations towards the language play an important role in the ideology of Basque sociolinguistics. Despite the predominance of individualistic ideology, the subject of Basque is treated as a group issue. On the one hand, while the decision to use and learn Basque is presented as a choice that individuals can make freely, several pro-Basque associations (e.g., the Council of Basque Social Organizations) often talk about the "violation of the right" to speak Basque. On the other, by participating in reflections and initiatives about minority languages, they are focusing on the group, and not so much on individual rights. They also talk about the "People of the Basque language," but the problem is that what exactly is meant by the "People of the Basque language" is not very clear. Does speaking or knowing the same language make us a group? Reflecting on these questions is very important for the future of the Basque language. The initial perspective on the construction of ideology about the Basque language will have different consequences for the language. And, furthermore, the way we understand groups may, in itself, reflect our position in the individualist-collectivist debate.

The non-normalization of the Basque language can be seen as the result of oppression. In this case, we are talking about a structural phenomenon which we understand occurs as a result of institutionalized processes (David, 2014; Williams, 2012). In this perspective, the emphasis is on the group, and it is understood that in order to change the state of the language, structural changes are needed. Individual attitudes are viewed in the context of structure, and it is clear that even people who have made an obvious choice and are highly motivated to support Basque on a personal level will encounter structural difficulties in their desire to live their lives in Basque. On the other hand, from an individualistic point of view, no structural oppression is perceived, and, so, it is understood that the key to changing individual attitudes is to achieve changes in internal individual motivations. Therefore, the Basque language must be made attractive to individuals, and this will motivate them to speak it. Ergo, if structural obstacles did not exist, the use of Basque could be normalized.

In this case, if individuals who speak Basque form a collection of individuals that share a common language, according to Cudd's definition of social groups, they would not encounter any common social constraints, and, ultimately, would not form a social group per se. On the other hand, if we understand the situation of the language to be the result of oppression, those who speak Basque form a social group because its members, whether or not they are aware of it, are subject to social constraints as a social group.

There are many pro-Basque language initiatives in the Basque Country. For example, there are five fundraising festivals for Ikastola schools (*Kilometroak, Nafarroa Oinez, Herri Urrats, Ibilaldia*, and *Araba Euskaraz*) held annually throughout the entire Basque Country. In addition, *Korrika* marches are held every two years which, like the Ikastola events, attract huge crowds. The news reports the popularity of the events highlighting the thousands of Basque speakers who join together to support the Basque language. The question, however, is whether sharing an interest in the Basque language makes one part of a group or not. Does being in favor of the Basque language mean that we are members of a single social group? Are we the *people of the Basque language*?

7. Basque language and scientific debates

"Nobody shrinks," said Treehorn's father.
"Well, I'm shrinking," said
Treehorn. "Look at me."
F.P. Heide. *The shrinking of Treehorn.*

The idea of the antiquity of the Basque language is widespread among Basques. If we know anything about the Basque language, it is that its origins are unknown. It is a pre-Indo-European language and has no clear connection with any other language or family of languages. We Basque speakers share a deep-seated idea that our language is "unique." This is not something only scientists and linguists are aware of; everyone in the Basque Country believes it.

Much research in the areas of linguistics, history, anthropology, and archaeology has attempted to shed light on the obscure origins and evolution of the Basque language. The findings have entered the public consciousness, and certain "facts" about the origins and history of the language are popular knowledge.

In his research on the phenomenon of social representations, Moscovici (1984) established a distinction between abstract scientific ideas and popularized commonsense ideas. He suggested ways of studying how scientific ideas become commonsense ideas, based on making scientific ideas in psychoanalysis widely known (Moscovici, 2008; Billig, 2008). According to Moscovici, in order to study the subject, it is important to refer to the origins of these scientific ideas. For example, to examine the ideas of psychoanalytical theory on its route to common sense, we can turn to Freud's early formulations. Billig does not see the distinction between scientific ideas and commonsense ideas in the same way as Moscovici does. By examining the origins of the ideas of psychoanalysis, Billig demonstrates that the use of several concepts that have spread into popular usage can be traced back to initial scientific formulations. For example, in Moscovici's view, the original theoretical meaning of the concept "complex" changed as it became popular in everyday conversation. Billig, on the other hand, sees this view of the transfer of ideas as too simple, and explains the different ways the term "complex" was used by Freud and Jung when formulating their theories of psychoanalysis. He mentions the controversy the term led to among the early psychoanalysts, and, therefore, denies that abstract scientific ideas change their meaning when they become social representations.

> To attribute this change in the meaning of 'complex' just to the journey from science to social representation may be historically too simple. Freud, in his 'History of the Psychoanalytic Movement,' complained about the way that Jung had popularized the word 'complex.' (Billig, 2008, p.360)

According to this view, scientific ideas and commonsense ideas are both controversial.

More than a decade has passed since a controversy about the history of the Basque language began, and it continues to this day. It is an interesting example of how a scientific debate on a subject can transcend the scientific sphere and enter the public arena. It can be analyzed from the perspective of a discursive moment in the construction of the history of the Basque language, and one in which scientific ideologies and popular common sense interacted in this construction.

In 2006, a team of archaeologists was involved in excavating a site known as Iruña-Veleia (Iruña de Oca), located ten kilometers from Vitoria-Gasteiz (Araba). The site features the ruins of a Bronze Age settlement (ca. 1000 BC) which was later occupied by the Romans. It had been a prosperous town during the first two centuries AD but fell into decline in the third century following the fall of the Roman Empire. It was eventually abandoned in the sixth century. Archaeologists began excavating the site in the late nineteenth century, and work has continued since then. The team at work on the site in 2006 was led by archaeologist Eliseo Gil who had been working there since 1994.

In 2006, samples of graphite were found in remnants of writings and drawings (mainly on ceramics, but also on bone and brick) which were considered "exceptional" and "unusual." The appearance of graphite in Roman-era sites is not uncommon, but these findings were considered to be "uncommon."

The head of the dig, along with several researchers from the University of the Basque Country, held a press conference in June 2006 to announce the findings. The Latin religious graffiti placed the arrival of Christianity in the Basque Country a century earlier than previously thought.

At the second press conference, several items of graffiti on ceramics were announced. They included words and phrases written in ancient Basque. The joy of the discovery did not last long because a number of scientists and experts began to question whether the findings were authentic or not. The controversy spread beyond the scientific community and caused a stir among the wider public.

It became a debate as to whether these remains were authentic or had been forged. Everyone wanted to find the "truth." Those who regarded the discovery as fake sought to prove so and presented supporting arguments; and the archaeologists who had made the discovery presented counter-arguments to rebut the criticism they were subjected to. Both sides believed that the "truth" could be found in science. Among those who believed the findings were false were two vociferous linguists from the University of the Basque Country; they argued from a linguistic perspective that the writing on these pieces of pottery had been forged. The archaeologists responsible for the discoveries demanded archaeometric tests be carried out, arguing that the issue could only be settled thus, and the "truth" would come out. These tests were never carried out.

In this discussion, the people who considered the graffiti to be fake mainly used linguistic arguments to defend their position. They mentioned anachronisms, spelling mistakes, the presence of letters that did not exist at the time, as well as issues to do with the structure of the language. Those who did not consider the graffiti to be fake offered counter-arguments to this linguistic criticism (Elexpuru, 2018). The argument in favor of turning to archaeology and using archaeometric methods to find out the "truth" was also highly significant. Not only did the archaeologists involved in the dig (Lurmen company) call for this solution, but so did a grassroots movement which was founded to get to the bottom of the Iruña-Veleia case:

> Lurmen has always been in favor of conducting any tests that could clear up any questions about the inscriptions. . . . And we have seen that dating the artefacts is the main demand of the pro-enlightenment movement. (Elexpuru, 2018, p. 81)

In this particular argument, the issue of who will ultimately reveal the "truth" becomes fundamental: philologists or archaeologists. Both groups accept that a "truth" is being sought, and that "truth" can be achieved by scientific means. It is debatable, however, which branch of science should be used to arrive at this "truth."

In an interview in *Berria* on March 3, 2009, the University of the Basque Country (EHU) researchers Gorrotxategi and Lakarra stated that they had arrived at the "truth" through linguistics and maintained that the findings were most certainly fake. They advocated in favor of the supremacy of philology over archaeology in order to reach the "truth" in the debate (*Berria*, March 3, 2009):

> "Some are still wondering if the pieces are real," explained Gorrotxategi. "More tests need to be carried out in the lab to determine the patina. . . but that would be starting off in the wrong direction. What is under debate? Texts. Who should say what needs to be said about texts? Philologists. And what the philologists say has to be accepted." Joseba Lakarra, next to him, agreed without hesitation. "We are sure."

The "Iruña-Veleia affair" has turned into a kind of mystery/horror saga. Juan Martín Elexpuru, PhD in Basque Philology, wrote a book entitled *¿Qué está pasando con*

Iruña-Veleia? (What is going on with Iruña-Veleia?, 2018) on the "veracity" of the graffiti and the movement that emerged as a result of the controversy. The book details the publications, conferences, and lectures held on the subject over the years, quoting a litany of Basque and international researchers. A debate within a specialized world has also become a debate in society at large. From the outset, the scientific community and popular commonsense community both joined in the controversy.

A considerable number of graffiti were found. According to the archaeologists who made the discovery, it was most likely to have been educational in nature. The material, which appears in Latin, Greek, Egyptian, and Basque, discusses mythology and features the names of philosophers, emperors, kings, politicians, and other figures (Elexpuru, 2018).

The prestigious Bermudian doctor in archaeology Edward Harris (famous for developing the Harris Matrix method) wrote in an article about Iruña-Veleia:

> As for the extraordinary variety of skills and knowledge that would be needed to produce the 400 "forgeries" discussed, the archaeologists at Iruña-Veleia would be among the most prominent geniuses in modern archaeology and should be given the best professorships in the land instead of being expelled from their profession by those whose motivation escapes the imagination. (*GARA*, November 18, 2015)

Harris argues that archaeological methods will clarify the debate. He argues that by using these methods, the "truth" can be obtained, and is astonished that existing archaeological methods were not used in this case.

Following the controversy over the findings, the supporters of those who considered the findings "fake" took the case to court. By doing so, the discussion was not limited to a scientific discussion or to an interdisciplinary discussion. Elexpuru quotes Lakarra:

> Even before the end of June 2006, it had ceased to be a scientific problem to become another of a very different nature: police and the judiciary, on the one hand, and historiography on the other. (Elexpuru, 2018, p. 19)

In this way, whether or not the subject should be clarified in the field of science, or whether the "truth" should be reached through a trial, also became a matter of debate. At the trial in February 2020, the judge deemed the graffiti to be fake. The judge gave his "truth," which, of course, had consequences for the archaeologists who had worked at the excavations.

However, this "truth" did not mean that the controversy was over. In fact, it has continued, the accused arguing that the methods offered by archaeology should be used to seek the "truth." From the linguists' point of view, the debate is over: the "truth" has emerged, and there is no need to continue the argument. The point, from a rhetorical perspective, is that a "truth" always has the potential to turn into a controversy, but for that to happen, both sides must be willing to reason. Not joining an argument, Billig explains, can be a rhetorical strategy:

> The refusal to enter a debate can itself be a rhetorical strategy, based upon the recognition that the mere act of answering a question imparts legitimacy to the question. (Billig, 1987, p. 222)

The proportions the debate took on and the consequences of all these controversies may be connected to the fact that archaeological discoveries and their interpretations are an important factor in the construction of collective memory. As Middleton and Edwards point out in their book *Collective Remembering*:

> The "truth" of the past is always, at least potentially, at issue. It is not to be found unambiguously deposited in some objective social record or archive, nor yet as infinitely malleable in the service of the present. It obtains neither as "fact" nor "invention," but as an epistemological enterprise, created in dialectic and argument between those contrary positions. (Middleton & Edwards, 1990b, p. 9)

Interpretations of the "unusual" graffiti finds at Iruña-Veleia can construct collective memory in one particular direction or in another. Collective memory and ideology are intertwined. Constructed collective pasts ultimately lay the foundations for the future in rhetorical terms. Michael Billig talks about the connection between ideology and social memory:

> Ideology itself will be a form of social memory, in as much as it constitutes what collectively is remembered and also what is forgotten or what aspects of society's history continue to be commemorated and what are relegated to the unread archives. In this way, memory will be both a part of ideology, as well as being a process by which ideology, and thereby the power relations of society, are reproduced. (Billig, 1990, p. 60)

Collective memory is not limited to the interpretation of a particular historical series of events, as Billig argues: Through collective memory, a group can "remember" its common history (Billig, 1990, p. 62). In this sense, interpretations of many archaeological finds can strengthen or weaken a group's collective memory, ideology, or power.

In the case of the Iruña-Veleia findings, taking them to be "fake" or accepting the possibility that they may be "authentic" leads to different interpretations of history. According to Elexpuru, this has been at the heart of the controversy:

> It is a fairly widespread opinion - which I share - that if Basque had not appeared, this monumental muddle would not have taken place, and that the rest of the pieces would have received the approval of the scientific community. (Elexpuru, 2018, p. 19)

Such findings occur in a rhetorical context, and their interpretation is conditioned by that context. In terms of rhetoric, it is ideological, and depending on the ideologies that may be in dispute, the same findings can be interpreted in one way or another. In interpreting the past of the Basque language, ideology is constructed to understand the Basque of the present and the Basque of the future.

In this sense, the discoveries of Iruña-Veleia are part of a wider controversy. The theory of "Late Basquification" is put into question if these findings are authentic. According to various theories, when the Romans arrived in the Basque Country, the Autrigones, Caristii, Varduli and Berones who lived in Araba, Bizkaia, Gipuzkoa, and La Rioja respectively were not Basque, but Indo-European.

According to this theory, the Basques were Vascones and Aquitani and would have arrived in the modern-day regions of Araba, Bizkaia, and Gipuzkoa at a later date. Other historians, on the other hand, question the "Late Basquification" theory.

Jeanine Czubaroff speaks of the "deliberative" nature of strategic scientific debates (Czubaroff, 1989). Based on "codified-law argumentation" and "common-law argumentation" as differentiated in Toulmin's *Human Understanding* (1972), she develops the two concepts. In the first, she explains that there is an implicit agreement on the theoretical framework, concepts, and methods, and so the discussion takes place within that conceptual theoretical framework. In the second, however, the disagreements under discussion tend to go deeper. As Czubaroff puts it, "conceptual questions and disagreements are at the heart of strategic scientific debates" (Czubaroff, 1989, p. 29).

In this sense, when these types of scientific debates occur, basic theoretical, conceptual, and methodological frameworks are questioned. She notes that major problems arise in these types of discussions:

> Serious problems arise when scientists do not share strategic agreements. Frequently, the discourse between opponents is strident, dogmatic, and at cross purposes, with each side offering empirical or formal arguments which from their perspective make sense, but which are unconvincing or irrelevant to their opponents. (Czubaroff, 1989 p. 28)

The Iruña-Veleia scientific debate can be classified as belonging to this type of strategic debate. The theoretical frameworks of the two sides are in direct conflict. The discussion was not an explicit theoretical framework discussion, but, rather, centered on the "veracity" vs. "falsity" of the graffiti. In fact, a scientific debate was not really developed. On the one hand, there is an implicit acceptance of the ideas in the "Late Basquification" theory framework, while on the other, the archaeologists accept the possibility that the "Late Basquification" framework may be questionable. It is true that a debate never took place on "Late Basquification" vs. "Early Basquification," but the whole Iruña-Veleia controversy brought these questions to light.

Either construction of the past of the Basque language will construct its future ideologically in one direction or another. The language "truths" about the past will condition the "truths" about the present and the future of the language. They are ideological truths from a rhetorical perspective.

8. The rhetorical dimension of ethnolinguistic vitality

Rhetoricians can so readily reverse apparent meanings because real meanings are so reversible.
K.Burke. *The war of words.*

The concept of ethnolinguistic vitality was introduced in 1977 by Giles, Bourhis, and Taylor. These authors aimed to study the complex relationships between different language groups. As intergroup relationships occur in a context, they identify several sociostructural factors that condition group vitality and argue that combinations of these structural variables will affect the life force of an ethnolinguistic group and can be classified into three groups: *Status*, *demographic*, and *institutional support* factors. Variables within the status set are related to the prestige of the language group. The variables included in the demographic set are connected with the number and territorial distribution of the group members. Finally, the institutional support variables are related to the formal and informal representation of language groups in institutions at national, regional, and community levels (Giles, Bourhis & Taylor, 1977).

By measuring the variables in the three groups and analyzing them in combination with each other, the authors classified the life force of language groups as low, medium, or high. Their theory was based on Tajfel's findings on intergroup relations (Tajfel, 1974) and Giles's speech accommodation theory (Giles, Taylor & Bourhis, 1973; Giles and Ogay, 2007). It has been four decades since they published this framework for the study of language relationships, and their ideas have been used in numerous studies. As is often the case, the authors, on seeing the limitations of their initial approach, which was considered an objective means of measuring ethnolinguistic vitality, developed a more advanced method which took more subjective factors into account. Therefore, in order to measure the vitality of a group—apart from measuring the objective vitality of the group for status, demographic, and institutional data—tools have also been designed to measure its subjective vitality (Bourhis, Giles & Rosenthal, 1981; Bourhis and Sachdev, 1984). For example, experts have used questionnaires to measure perceptions of vitality, which they have changed and amended to include nuances over the decades (Abrams, Barker & Giles, 2009; Ehala, 2009).

The research framework for the study of relationships between language groups has also had an impact on the situation of the Basque language. Several studies on Basque have been carried out using this theoretical framework (Cenoz and Valencia, 1993; Romay, Garcia-Mira & Azurmendi, 1999).

This theoretical framework for the study of language relationships seeks, as mentioned before, to take the context and sociostructural factors of the languages into account. As the authors claim, combinations of these structural factors provide us with a context for understanding the vitality of ethnolinguistic groups:

> It is our contention that these three types of structural variables interact to provide the context for understanding the vitality of ethnolinguistic groups. (Giles, Bourhis & Taylor, 1977, p. 310)

Since I understand that sociostructural factors are rhetorical in nature, I believe that some of the ideas underlying the concept of ethnolinguistic vitality require further reflection.

Firstly, social structures are social processes. It is vitality, or life force, that determines a group's survival. I understand this strength or vitality as an ongoing process, rather than as something possessed. As Joseba Ariznabarreta states in *Pueblo y Poder. Cuadernos para la reconstrucción de la razón* (People and Power. Notes for the Reconstruction of Reason, 2007), the power a group exerts is immeasurable. When trying to quantify power, we always come across qualitative aspects which cannot be quantified. When ethnolinguistic vitality is measured, be it objectively or subjectively, this vitality is classified as high, medium, or low. I view power, or vitality, as a process, and as such, something that takes place within a relationship. To the extent to which it is a social phenomenon, it is a process that takes place in a rhetorical argumentative context. When examining objective vitality in order to measure the ethnolinguistic vitality of a language and the subjective vitality perceived by speakers, I believe that this rhetorical argumentative context is ignored. I believe that to say that a language has an objective vitality—measurable through variables related to status, demographics, and institutional protection—denies the rhetorical nature of the language and group power variables. In terms of status, for example, when we examine the explanations for all the variables related to status, we come across some which are objectively immeasurable. For example, Giles, Bourhis, and Taylor take into account the self-esteem of the language group in connection with the social status of the language:

> This refers to the degree of esteem a linguistic group affords itself; often, this amount of group self-esteem closely resembles that attributed by the outgroup. (Giles, Bourhis & Taylor, 1977, p. 310)

I believe it is impossible to measure a group's self-esteem objectively. When presenting these measurements, each researcher's rhetoric comes into play. When one measurement is termed "objective" and another "subjective," for example, it becomes clear that the author's rhetorical position is involved. As Simons reminds us regarding the rhetoric of research work:

> Broadly speaking, virtually all scholarly discourse is rhetorical in the sense that issues need to be named and framed, facts interpreted and conclusions justified; furthermore, in adapting arguments to ends, audiences, and circumstances, the writer (or speaker) must adopt a persona, choose a style, and make judicious use of what Kenneth Burke has called the "resources of ambiguity" in language. (Simons, 1990a, p. 9)

Over their long careers, given the limitations involved in the objective measurement of the vitality of language groups in intergroup relationships, researchers in the field began to carry out the subjective measurements mentioned earlier. My second reflection on the ethnolinguistic vitality research framework, therefore, is that subjective measurements are also problematic.

To gain a subjective view of the vitality of a language group, a questionnaire aimed at capturing the group members' perceptions was designed using the most advanced tools available at the time (Bourhis, Giles

& Rosenthal, 1981; Abrams, Barker & Giles, 2009). Paradoxically, this theoretical framework which aimed to highlight the importance of sociostructural factors, focused on the individual when it came to obtaining data, and I maintain that vitality researchers understand individuals to be free from sociostructural factors. I also believe that human thought and subjective opinion are situated within a context. Therefore, when people fill in questionnaires containing variables on the vitality of language, they take positions on issues that are debated within the context of a particular historical period. The subject interprets the context by taking positions about different ideological frameworks. The questionnaires used by the researchers to study the subjective perceptions of the vitality of the language group appear to exclude the study of the ideological framework from the research. Using such questionnaires limits the respondents' opportunity to give reasons and justify their "opinion" on the contextual ideological framework. The complexity of the matter is not reflected. For instance, Giles, Bourhis, and Taylor mentioned in their initial proposal on the concept of ethnolinguistic vitality, the fact that groups have a negative self-image does not necessarily mean that they will institute change. As the authors state, the groups would need to be aware of the existence of an alternative:

> They must also be aware, or become aware, that cognitive alternatives to the existing status relationship between it and the superior group are possible. (Giles, Bourhis & Taylor, 1977, p. 319)

Therborn, in his book *The Ideology of Power and the Power of Ideology* (1980), discusses the ideological formation of human subjects and refers to three fundamental modes of ideological interpellation. Firstly, through ideology, subjects recognize what exists and what does not. Secondly, they recognize what is good, fair, attractive, or against their interests. And finally, they recognize what is possible and impossible (Therborn, 1980, p. 18).

From this point of view, unlike that of vitality researchers, people's views about a particular group's situation and potential alternatives to that situation are connected to ideologies. People's subjective thinking is not an individual internal cognitive process, but rather a position argued in relation to ideologies.

As ideology researchers have often pointed out, ideological concepts have a long and complex history, which, as I have said before, has been understood in different ways (McLellan, 1995; Thompson, 1984). In their book *Ideological Dilemmas*, Billig and his colleagues refer to two meanings which are often ascribed to the concept of ideology: lived ideology and intellectual ideology:

> There is first of all "lived ideology," which refers to ideology as a society's way of life. This sort of ideology includes what passes for common sense within a society. On the other hand, there is an "intellectual ideology," which is a system of political, religious or philosophical thinking and, as such, is very much the product of intellectuals or professional thinkers. (Billig et al, 1988, p. 27)

Therborn, for example, incorporates both intellectual ideology and notions of everyday life—common sense—into the concept of ideology:

> Thus, the conception of ideology employed here deliberately includes both everyday notions and 'experience' and elaborate intellectual doctrines, both the 'consciousness' of social actors and the institutionalized thought-systems and discourses of a given society. (Therborn, 1980, p. 2)

In any case, when it comes to the study of human thought and opinions, instead of finding isolated cognitive products of individuals, we come across ideologies, and dialectical processes between ideology and people's thinking which must be taken into account when considering any social phenomenon. As Therborn says in the preface to his book *The Ideology of Power and the Power of Ideology*:

> The actual operation of ideology in contemporary society is better illustrated by the cacophony of sounds and signs of a big city street than by the text serenely communicating with the solitary reader, or the teacher or TV-personality addressing a quiet domesticated audience. (Therborn, 1980, p.vii)

People are born, raised, and live immersed in a sea of ideologies. By this I do not mean that we receive ideas that flow in a single direction and live with them. Billig and his colleagues, for example, have reflected on the link between the formal ideological system and informal common sense. Moscovici's studies also describe how the concepts of science are represented in common sense, as I mentioned in the previous chapter (Moscovici, 1984; 2008). From the perspective of Billig and his colleagues, this transfer of ideas is not unidirectional:

> The passage needs not be unidirectional, going from intellectual discourse to mass discourse. The reverse journey is also made, as intellectuals take up the concepts of everyday life and embellish them in their theorizing. (Billig et al, 1988, p. 26)

In the same way, Therborn also argues that ideological processes take place in different directions:

> Ideologies not only subject people to a given order. They also qualify them for conscious social action, including actions of gradual or revolutionary change. Ideologies do not function merely as "social cement." (Therborn, 1980, p.vii)

So when people think about ideologies, they are already immersed in them and constrained by their limitations, and construct their thoughts accordingly:

> In analysing the ideological representation of dilemmas in modern consciousness, we are not viewing individual thinkers as blindly following the dictates of ideological schemata. We see them thinking, but within the constraints of ideology, and with the elements of ideology. (Billig et al, 1988, p. 27)

As several authors have said, moreover, ideologies should not be understood as coherent systems of ideas: they are inherently controversial. Billig, for example, reminds us of the dilemmatic aspect of ideology (considering both lived ideology and intellectual ideology), and the contrary elements of thought:

> In fact, many of the conventional images of ideology assume that thinking is non-dilemmatic. They tend to treat ideological systems as integrated systems of thinking, or, to use a current psychological term, as schemata par excellence. Therefore, the passage from intellectual ideology to everyday ideology is often assumed to be one in which an elitely constructed consistency is imposed upon mass thinking, with the result that ideological consistency becomes socially diffused. Our approach, with its emphasis upon the dilemmatic aspects, questions this image, for it focuses upon the contrary elements of thinking. (Billig et al, 1988, p. 27)

The complex interactions between ideology and individual ideas show us the importance of placing these *subjective* measurements in context.

This image of the complexity of ideologies allows us to form an idea of the complexity of institutions. My third reflection, then, is on the institution variable as a basis for the concept of ethnolinguistic vitality.

As a language's institutional presence increases, researchers using the theory of vitality argue that this also increases. Among the institutions they mention are government, churches, education, industry, media, and culture:

> The vitality of a linguistic minority seems to be related to the degree its language is used in various institutions of the government, church, business and so forth. (Giles, Bourhis & Taylor, 1977, p. 309)

With regard to the formal and informal support for languages in national, regional, or community institutions, the authors state that:

> Institutional support refers to the degree of formal and informal support a language receives in the various institutions of a nation, region or community (Breton, 1971). Informal support refers to the extent to which a minority has organized itself in terms of pressure groups. . . . It is suggested that a linguistic minority is vital to the extent that its language and group members are well-represented formally and informally in a variety of institutional settings. (Giles, Bourhis & Taylor, 1977, p. 315)

They attach special importance to the presence of language in formal education. In the case of the Basque language, from the creation and expansion of the Ikastola movement until today, the presence of the language in education has grown, and today it is predominant in many parts of the Basque Country.

However, this does not allow a direct interpretation of the vitality of Basque. To do this, we need to add some details about the concept of institutions. This has been widely studied in the social sciences. In fact, social groups are institutionalized groups. The term "institution" is often used to refer only to modern organizations (Berthod, 2016; Jepperson, 1991; Zucker, 1983). However, a broader conceptualization of the term institutions describes them as the most general, universal development in the history of human society (Eisenstadt, 1968; Jepperson, 1991; Tomasello et al, 2009). A social group comes into being through an institutionalization process and reproduces itself in the same way. At the same time, social groups disappear when the institutionalized patterns of behavior for reproducing them are deinstitutionalized (Tolbert and Zucker, 1996). Following Scott's conception of institutions, every institution is based on three pillars:

> Institutions comprise regulative, normative and cultural-cognitive elements that, together with associated activities and resources, provide stability and meaning to social life. (Scott, 2014, p. 56)

According to Scott, the cultural-cognitive aspect of institutions is related to a symbolically constructed social we-ness, as this pillar has constitutive functions. It is located in the "taken for granted" end of the continuum from the "conscious to the unconscious" (Scott, 2014, p. 59). The constitutive function of the cultural-cognitive pillar is of fundamental importance as symbolic processes work to construct social reality, creating frames and patterns of thought and action. Constitutive rules construct the social objects and events to which regulative rules are applied (Scott, 2014). Every social group institutionalizes its pattern of behavior on the basis of the common understanding of "who" the group is and what the meaning of that particular identity is. Constitutive rules are so basic to social structure, so fundamental to life in society, that they are often overlooked (Berger and Luckmann, 1967; Schneider, 1976; Scott, 2014).

It is precisely the cognitive-cultural pillar that I associate with ideology. As I have said, people live immersed in a sea of ideologies, and these ideologies help us to recognize what exists, what is good, and what is possible. These ideologies are present in the foundation of institutions. Therefore, institutions are not only what we see in the open. When vitality researchers refer to pressure groups, they are talking about informal organizations. From our point of view, they are institutional processes that take place on different ideological bases. These institutional processes clash with other institutional processes that are being built on other ideological foundations, and a power struggle ensues. Social groups may differ in their degree of institutionalization; in other words, they may vary in the equilibrium between the three basic pillars. This equilibrium is related to the effective power that the group exercises.

Institutions are dynamic processes that are constantly under construction and deconstruction, and our social world is a "sea" of institutions, and, consequently, of ideologies. From this perspective, it follows that institutions are not the only complex organizations that the modern world has given us. Specifically, vitality researchers have paid special attention to the pressure they define as being applied informally.

While these researchers may appear to attribute certain importance to these informal social pressures, in fact they measure vitality by measuring the presence of the language in more formal, consolidated institutions.

> At a more formal level, it would seem that groups which have little representation at the decision-making levels of State, business and cultural affairs would be less able to survive as distinctive linguistic entities than those who have organized themselves as political entities seeking permanent representation at the State's legislative and executive levels. (Giles, Bourhis & Taylor, 1977, p. 316)

In this view, the controversial nature of states and other institutions is not taken into account. It seems that there *are* states and state structures, and that a presence in these structures conditions a group's vitality. However, in our view, in many relationships between language groups, the ideological basis of this institutional reality lies at the heart of the controversy. There may be conflicting ways of institutionalizing groups in language-contact situations, and taking institutional reality for granted is a rhetorical position which researchers may need to reflect on. Several researchers have criticized the ethnolinguistic vitality theory (Yagmur and Ehala, 2011). For example, Husband and Saifullah Khan argue that the concept of ethnolinguistic vitality is defined in terms of the dominant group criterion (Husband and Saifullah Khan, 1982), and Tollefson's critique also points in that direction (Tollefson, 1991). Furthermore, Husband and Saifullah Khan point out that vitality researchers do not take into account that these institutions are built from the dominant group's perspective, and that therefore minority ethnic group schools, religious schools, etc., may be under the control of the dominant group.

The mere presence of the Basque language in educational institutions does not indicate the vitality of the Basque language, as the trajectory of the Ikastola movement shows. Quantification itself is a rhetorical concept. What is quantified? And how is it quantified? According to Urla and Burdick, one of the characteristics of the quantification of Basque is that there are multiple sources for quantification:

> One of the distinctive and enduring features of the Basque case is that data gathering comes not only from government offices, but also come

> from a plethora of public and private entities. . . . Quantification is being produced by multiple entities, from the very local Basque language group, cultural associations, and schools, to large interregional collaborations. (Urla & Burdick, 2018, p. 76)

The Basque Sociolinguistic Survey, for example, is a quinquennialsurvey which was set up in 1990 and about which Urla and Burdick say, "in contrast to the census, which is restricted to the Basque Autonomous Community and Navarre, [this survey] reports on the broader territory of Basque speakers residing in what are considered to be the seven historic provinces of Euskal Herria" (Urla and Burdick, 2018, p. 77). Therefore, the basis for the type of quantification may encompass different ideologies.

The pro-Basque movement has also paid special attention to the street surveys that have measured the use of Basque in everyday life in the seven Basque provinces because the presence of the language in the aforementioned institutions did not necessarily reflect the use of Basque which the movement aspired to (Urla and Burdick, 2018). I believe that it is important to bear in mind the nature and the ideological basis of the process of institutionalization when attempting to understand the social phenomenon and/or the vitality of a language.

9. The evolution of discourse

When, finally, I turn on my radio and hear that in Africa forced labor has been inaugurated and legalized, I say that we have certainly been lied to: Hitler is not dead.
F. Fanon. *Black Skin, White Masks.*

When the subject of Basque and Basque identity is studied in social psychology, the death of Spanish dictator Francisco Franco (in 1975) is often used as a milestone because, immediately afterwards, changes in the Spanish state led to the establishment of the Basque Autonomous Community (BAC) and the Autonomous Community of Navarre (ACN) (Azurmendi and Martínez de Luna, 2011). The founding of the autonomous communities in Spain has been widely hailed as marking the beginning of democracy and freedom in the land. Many scholars have also interpreted it as a landmark event for the revitalization of important elements of Basque national identity (such as the language and other cultural expressions). The Basque language and culture were no longer banned and repressed and began to be officially recognized (Azurmendi, Larrañaga & Apalategi, 2008; Azurmendi and Martínez de Luna, 2011; Larrañaga, Garcia, Azurmendi & Bourhis, 2016).

The use of this landmark, however, also has a rhetorical dimension. In fact, it could be reasonably deduced that the dictator's death led to a change in the power relations of the time. Nevertheless, in politics and social relations, changes in form do not necessarily coincide with changes in power relations. The lack of overt conflict does not necessarily imply the absence of conflict. Scholars analyzing "power" have specified that there are often "latent" conflicts of interest which, of course, are not "peaceful" situations. A latent conflict "consists in a contradiction between the interests of those exercising power and the real interests of those they exclude" (Lukes, 2005).

During the dictatorship (1936–1975), no other language overshadowed Spanish, which was held as supreme by the dominant ideology. Torrealdai examined the discourse of the ruling class on the Basque language in the early years of the Franco regime, and published the results in the magazine *Jakin* (Torrealdai, 1982). He examined the laws, events, research, opinions, rules, and orders published of the period, and, bearing in mind what was being said and done to the Basque language at the time, it is not surprising that he titled his article *Euskararen zapalkuntza 1936-1939* (The oppression of the Basque language, 1936-1939). Torrealdai uses the term "cultural genocide" to describe what happened to the Basque language and culture. In one passage he explains why he focused on this particular period:

> The choice was simply to delimit the work. It does not suggest in any way, for example, that oppression only took place during those years, or that the oppression that took place then was identical to what had gone on before. The chosen time frame has a significant advantage, however: cultural genocide appeared "à l'état pur" during those years, in a pure state, laid bare, whereas, in later years, it would be covered up. (Torrealdai, 1982, p. 9)

What Torrealdai mentions in this passage is very important. It tells us that power relations based on oppression can take on different forms, in the same way hidden forms of modern racism have been observed by several experts on the subject. Many have used the concept of symbolic racism (Kinder and Sears, 1981; McConahay and Hough, 1976) to look at new forms of racism:

> *Symbolic racism* is the expression by suburban whites in terms of abstract ideological symbols and symbolic behaviors of the feeling that blacks are violating cherished values and making illegitimate demands for changes in the racial status quo. (McConahay & Hough, 1976, p. 23)

In their work, these researchers reflect the idea that racism can appear under many different guises:

> It is not the racism of the red-neck bigots of old who spewed forth hatred, doctrines of racial inferiority, and support for de jure segregation. Though these bigots might also engage in symbolic racism, our concern is with the racism of those who are both sociologically and psychologically "the gentle people of prejudice." (McConahay & Hough, 1976, p. 24)

Billig also mentions that racism can have explicit and implicit forms:

> 'Modern racism', unlike the old uninhibited racism, is expressed in covert ways, which avoid a direct appeal to racial values. Acts of discrimination and the voicing of prejudice will be justified in

> terms of any value but a racial one. The modern racists, unlike those of former times, will not express opposition, in principle, to a black person marrying a white one, but they will believe that "blacks are getting too demanding in their push for equal rights." (Billig, 1987, p. 218)

Prejudices against the Basque language and culture have not always been expressed in the same way. The explicit discourse against the Basque language which was prevalent in Franco's time is never heard today. In this sense, things have changed, but, as with racism, it cannot be directly inferred that this kind of discourse has disappeared altogether. In some cases, it has shifted to the private domain, only rearing its head occasionally in the public arena. An example of this is a sports story which was picked up by several media outlets on June 30, 2020. Two players from the *Athletic Club Bilbao* soccerteam posted a message on social media announcing their departure from the team at the end of the season but adding that they would play their final match. The statement caused a stir because it was written in Basque. The comments underneath contained explicit discourse against the Basque language and the players received death threats.

Such explicit discourses, however, are not currently found in public discourse. Respect for linguistic and cultural diversity is the general discourse heard in public from politicians, in the media, and on the street. The point is that this consensus in favor of the value of cultural and linguistic diversity can be interpreted in different ways, just as the value of racial equality can be interpreted in many ways:

> The value of equality has been established as a common object of agreement, but is open to differing interpretations (Verba and Orren, 1985). Instead of eradicating the old racial feelings, the value of equality has absorbed them, thereby allowing a tortuous escape from the force of social taboo. As a result, the category of 'equality' acquires a new, and dangerously contrary, meaning. (Billig, 1987, p. 218)

In the Basque Country, we receive discourses in favor of bilingualism and multilingualism from the public institutions. The Basque sociolinguistic model is also based on this idea. Since the end of the Franco era, pro-bilingualism, multilingualism, and cultural diversity discourse has prevailed. As mentioned throughout this book, Basque language activists are trying to move towards the normalization of the language based on these ideas:

> The foundational discourse in which the central Basque sociolinguistic theory and its subsequent policies are grounded in (sic) is the highlighting of a bilingual (multilingual in more recent years) scenario as the wisest and linguistically most profitable state of affairs for the survival of Basque. Hence, according to this hypothesis, the normalization of Basque should not be aimed at the substitution of either of the two majority languages Basque is in (uneven) contact with. (Ariznabarreta, 2019, p. 94)

Among languages, therefore, the idea of a conflict-free situation has dominated public discourse. In the cartoon

Dora esploratzailea (*Dora the Explorer*), which is broadcast on Basque children's TV, Dora speaks Basque and English in a friendly, non-politically-charged model of how languages can be connected. By including Basque and English words in the same sentence (it is not clear which language is being taught), children are presented with an image of a harmonious, uncontroversial relationship between languages. They are allowed to speak whatever language they want, neither is considered superior to the other, and it is even OK to mix them all up.

Terms such as cultural genocide or oppression, as used by Torrealdai, have disappeared from public discourse. The question is whether the disappearance of these terms is a sign of the disappearance of cultural genocide itself. In *Rhetoric, Ideology and Social Psychology. Essays in Honor of Michael Billig*, Rosalind Gill wrote a chapter on sexism entitled *The resurgence of sexism and the disappearance of "sexism."* In it, she analyzes the decline of the concept of sexism:

> In this chapter I want to enquire into the disappearance of this term, arguing that—paradoxically—it indexes the very phenomenon of which it speaks. The gender inequalities and power relations are sadly not a sign that sexism no longer exerts any force in the world, but rather—I will argue—indicates the hegemony of contemporary post- and anti-feminist ideas, with their suggestion that gender is no longer significant in determining "life chances," and that "all the battles have been won." (Gill, 2014, p. 109)

Gill emphasizes the importance of a rhetorical approach to the study of sexism and reflects on the concept of a "new sexism," arguing that sexism is changing but not disappearing. She uses the ideas that Billig emphasizes in his work on *"new racism"* (Billig, 1988), as well as "his important emphasis on the 'banal' and taken-for-granted practices that play a part in sustaining ideologies" (Gill, 2014, p. 110).

The terminology used by Torrealdai would be considered "excessive" from the point of view of current mainstream ideology for defining the situation which the Basque language and culture find themselves in. This is probably because it takes for granted a stable, unchangeable way of interpreting "cultural genocide," "oppression," and, ultimately, "prejudice" against the Basques. While the violent events of the Franco era may merit the use of the terms "oppression" and "cultural genocide," the different forms of asymmetric power relations between cultures are not identified in this closed view of "oppression" or "prejudice." In the same way, Gill criticizes certain ways of conceptualizing sexism:

> The chapter also seeks to intervene into discussions of 'prejudice' to critique the taken-for-granted understanding of sexism as a unitary, unchanging 'thing' that inheres in a relatively stable stock of ideas, stereotypes and practices. Against this I will argue for a revitalized and properly discursive understanding of sexism as a dynamic, malleable and diverse range of situated representations, discourses, and practices of power. (Gill, 2014, p. 109)

Torrealdai used the "oppression" of the Basque language during the 1936-1939 period to describe violent discursive and non-discursive practices concerning the Basque language and culture including prohibitions and arrests. It is commonly believed that since Franco's death, there has been no need to talk about the "oppression of the Basque language"; yet Torrealdai himself was arrested when *Euskaldunon Egunkaria* (The Basques´ Newspaper) was closed in 2003 for, as he put it, defending the Basque language and culture.

However, returning to my main issue, my aim is to emphasize the different forms of power relations, particularly the more subtle, less prominent practices of discourse which are the ones that interest me most. To do so, it is worth examining some examples.

As I said before, messages denoting positive attitudes to the Basque language are commonly found throughout the Basque Country. For example, signs proclaiming *Euskaraz badakigu ("We speak Basque")* can be seen in many public buildings and shops. The supposed objective of these slogans is to encourage people to speak Basque; therefore, their use would seem to support the Basque language. However, in rhetorical response to the implicit pro-Basque stance of such messages, others have produced similar signs in Spanish (*"Hablamos español" – "We speak Spanish")*. In truth, when a sign says *We speak Basque*, everyone who walks in knows that the people there speak Basque *as well as* Spanish or French. There is no doubt as to whether they speak Spanish or French. Whether or not they speak Basque, however, is a different matter. So an attitude that supports Basque carries the implicit message that Basque, as a second language, is considered to be additional knowledge, whereas *We speak Spanish* signs challenge the power relationship between the two languages.

There is another interesting example which shows the asymmetrical relationship between the languages. It is well-documented that, in Franco's time, people were not allowed to give their children Basque names. In Torrealdai's article there is a reference to a decree from 1938:

> The morbid exacerbation in some provinces of regional sentiment must also be pointed out as the source of registration anomalies, which has led, in certain registers, to a good number of names which are not only in a language other than official Spanish, but also involve a meaning contrary to the UNITY of the fatherland. Such is the case in the Basque Country, for example, with the names of Iñaki, Kepa, Koldobika and others which carry with them an indisputable meaning of SEPARATISM. (Torrealdai, 1982, p. 28)

Many people were forced to give their children Spanish names, but once the ban was lifted, some of them were re-registered with Basque names. Although the ban on Basque names ended with Franco, the use of Basque names generated another controversy far more recently. The weekly magazine *Argia*published the following headline (June 14, 2019): "For the first time, Euskaltzaindia accepts gender-neutral names." The article goes on to explain how, in 2011, Euskaltzaindia published a list of boys' and girls' names. The fact that Euskaltzaindia had assigned genders to Basque names had caused controversy over the years as the brochure published by the feminist group Bilgune Feminista, *Izena eta izana* (*Name and Being*), attests. According to the article published in *Argia*, Euskaltzaindia had found the binary system of Basque names extremely difficult to implement and officially informed the Spanish Ministry of Justice in January 2018 that some Basque names are not exclusively male or female. In another

Argia article published on August 1, 2016, a journalist wrote, quoting a member of Euskaltzaindia: "Spanish law says that boys' and girls' names must be clearly differentiated. This requires a specific set of criteria, but it is still very difficult because some [Basque] names are toponyms while others are common nouns with no grammatical gender. They need to understand that it is a very complicated issue, and that we are in a quandary." The journalist added that many citizens agree that it is difficult or impossible to assign a gender to Basque names: it is very difficult, if not impossible, to find traces of penises or vaginas in toponyms or common nouns in a language with no grammatical genders. The journalist criticizes Euskaltzaindia, saying that, as a result of their list, parents were having trouble registering their children.

When Spanish law obliged Euskaltzaindia to make such a list, one culture was implicitly perceived as being superior to the other. The code of one culture—the distribution of words by gender—was being forced upon another. Words in Spanish have a gender, but in Basque they do not. Therefore, Euskaltzaindia was forced to invent a gender code. While language is no longer explicitly forbidden as it was in Franco's time, the notion of a Spanish-Basque language hierarchy still persists.

Regarding the ideological context of the Basque language, while the current discourse and prejudice against the Basque language is less explicit than in Franco's time, the same structural social phenomena that implicitly reveal the hierarchy between the languages still exist. Billig examines the subject of "race" to explain the variability and dynamism of common places derived from common sense. If we go back a century and look at the way race was spoken about in Western society and compare it with the same topic today, we can see that differences exist. At first sight, these differences could lead us to conclude that anti-racist discourse has prevailed. But, as Billig argues, things are not so simple:

> The old common places may not disappear entirely from social acceptability, and despite taboos, the reality of racism still persists in the modern world. Detached from their old value, some racist images, beliefs, and even feelings may now travel under the protection of acceptable, and formerly contrary values. (Billig, 1987, p. 217)

So even though there are changes in the discourse, it does not mean that racism has disappeared. Changes in discourse can occur, and certain topics can become taboo. In other words, just as the purity of race at one time could be defended openly, speaking in this way today would be met with rejection by the vast majority:

> Changes can occur comparatively quickly, with old "facts" about the strangeness of other races, appearing quite suddenly as strange as any foreigner had been imagined to be. (Billig, 1987, p. 217)

It is important to pay attention to the details of discourse in order to study any social phenomenon because the hidden can carry as much weight as the obvious in the evolution of discourse.

10 . Things which are not (said)

Social amnesia is society's repression of remembrance—society's own past.
R. Jacoby. *Social Amnesia.*

In an interview with Xan Aire (*EKE*, September 30, 2014), the *bertsolari* or Basque improvisational poet Miren Artetxe mentioned several subjects that bertsolaris avoid or silence in their work. She mentions, for instance, certain limitations regarding humor. For example, when singing to the audience, a verse that might be aimed at a bald or overweight man would not be aimed at an overweight woman. In this sense, it is clear that bertsolaris use self-censorship when it comes to gender. Similarly, many other issues are also either avoided or silenced.

From a feminist perspective, Freud's theory of psychoanalysis has received much criticism, and many have advocated re-reading his work from a feminist viewpoint (Moi, 1981; Ramas, 1980; Sayers, 1990). The re-reading of a case involving a woman called Ida Bauer—referred to by Freud as Dora—has become particularly well-known.

Dora's case has transcended the merely feminist context (Decker, 1999). Michael Billig revisited many of Freud's cases in his excellent book *Freudian Repression. Conversation Creating the Unconscious* (Billig, 1999). According to Billig, there is a gap at the heart of Freud's theory: Freud never actually explains how repression occurs (Billig, 1999). In order to fill this gap, Billig reformulates Freud's idea of repression. According to Billig, repression should not be understood as a mysterious internal process. He sees repression as a process related to language, and language as inherently expressive and repressive. He argues that as we develop language skills, we learn to repress:

> To become proficient speakers, we need to repress. The business of everyday conversation provides the skills for repressing, while at the same time, it demands that we practice those skills. (Billig, 1999, p. 1)

Billig argues that Freud and his followers did not pay enough attention to the small routine words that occur in conversations:

> So often, the attention is drawn to the unusual or to the "big" symbolism. Perhaps, it was these little words that held the key to repression. Through their use, speakers can switch the topics of talk almost imperceptibly. Maybe these same little words allow us to change the topics of our internal thoughts, thereby driving away uncomfortable desires. (Billig, 1999, p. 4)

From this perspective, Billig offers us an interesting reading of Freud's theory. Recognizing Freud's contribution to the idea of repression, he goes a step further by examining *how* repression is exercised. Throughout the book, he illustrates theoretical issues by re-reading the cases studied by Freud, and by analyzing some of Freud's own experiences.

In one of the book chapters, he examines Dora's case. In his examination of the details of Freud and Dora´s conversations and Freud's psychoanalytical interpretation of the case, Billig points out an aspect which is silent: the Jewish dimension:

> Freud and Dora found it easier to talk of the supposedly taboo topics of sex than they did of their own precarious circumstances as Jews in antisemitic Vienna. (Billig, 1999, p. 10)

Billig shows that even when Freud's work is re-read, many authors continue to reproduce these repressions, leaving some issues silent.

Although Billig acknowledges the contribution of feminists, when it comes to re-reading Freud's work, he does not concur with the feminist view of Freud. In these (feminist) critiques, Freud appears as a powerful man, a man who identifies with the patriarchal society of the time. It has been argued that he lacked political perspective in his psychoanalysis, which, in turn, contributed to the preservation of the patriarchal system. Billig identifies a key issue that remains silent throughout these critiques:

> However, something crucial is being omitted. Freud was not a comfortable member of his society. The description "educated, bourgeois male" neglects a category which was central to Freud's political and social position. He was a member of a much discriminated-against minority; and so was Dora. Ultimately both Freud and Dora were to be driven from their society in fear of their lives. (Billig, 1999, p. 221)

Regarding this key characteristic of Freud and Dora's, Billig uses a parallelism to illustrate the "strange" stance adopted by researchers who viewed Freud's work as lacking political perspective. He quotes the hypothetical case of a radical academic who examines the work of a black doctor living under Apartheid in South Africa, and who concludes that the doctor's reflections must be political. But Billig asks the question: Would we not be surprised if the academic failed to mention Apartheid, racial politics, or the fact that the doctor was black?

Billig explains the political atmosphere and historical context of the time, and goes on to identify a number of challenging experiences in Freud's and Dora's families. In Dora's case and Freud's reading of it, Billig points to their silence about their Jewishness and their ways of escaping from various related issues. He tells us about the dialectic of remembering and forgetting:

> The dialectic of remembering and forgetting can be examined in relation to language and dialogue. As one matter is spoken (or written) about, so others are kept from immediate dialogic attention. The dialogues of psychoanalysis need not be excluded. (Billig, 1999, p. 223)

Billig points out that in Freud and Dora's conversations, as well as in a report Freud later wrote about the case, they had avoided Jewish issues. Billig understands the avoidance of these issues as collective silences that go beyond their personal phobias.

From Freud's point of view, repression has a biological function, understood as a "resource" for living with the aggression and sexual impulses we have from birth. Billig, on the other hand, sees repression as dialogical, and not biological:

> But repression itself does not need to be understood in biological terms, if one assumes that socially inappropriate responses or thoughts, rather than biological urges, constitute the objects of repression. (Billig, 1999, p. 254)

From this point of view, therefore, the work of exposing what has been repressed is uninterrupted. From his biological point of view, Freud might have thought that he had done a great deal of work in revealing these specific desires. From Billig's perspective, there are endless issues that we can repress:

> There is no guarantee that what was repressed in one historical epoch will be repressed in another, as if the underlying forces always remained constant. Each moment of human history will produce its own restrictions. Consequently, the task of exploring the unsaid is endless. Ideological analysis, to adapt a Freudian phrase, should be an interminable analysis. (Billig, 1999, p. 254)

So, from Billig's point of view, what is said and what is not said needs to be examined in order to see what we are repressing in each context. In this way, he links repression to ideology:

> If repression is seen to be linked to language, rather than to sexual impulses, then there is less temptation to overlook its ideologically changing forms. (Billig, 1999, p. 258)

In order to study repression and the mechanisms used for implementing it, it is necessary to examine what is said and what is silenced depending on each period. Freud, who focused on the repression of sexuality and aggression, did not claim that this type of repression should be "liberated," but thought that it should be understood. In fact, he understood repression as a phenomenon which developed in order to maintain social life. Billig, by linking repression, language, and ideology, examines how certain issues become taboo at different times, while others come to light. Referring to Freud's time and current taboos, he mentions that many issues related to sexuality that were taboo back then are no longer taboo today, whereas the opposite has happened in the case of racism. Many of the things that were explicitly said in the past are now considered taboo. But, he emphasizes, when examining repression, one must go beyond external expressions:

> However, to ensure that the previous way of talking is tipped into the garbage can of history, it is not sufficient merely to prohibit certain forms of public utterances. Internal controls also have to be set in place, so that the thought, as much as the outwardly spoken act, becomes shameful. (Billig, 1999, p. 260)

From Billig's point of view, there is no conversation without repression. It is a mechanism that will always be used and adapted to the issues of the day. This reminds us that we also have a problem with ourselves:

> Not only does morality condition repression, but it should also condition the analysis of repression. A danger always stalks such analysis. As we talk about repression, so we are using language. We will be looking in a particular direction, unaware of

> what we are overlooking, unaware of our silences. Always there is more analysis to be done. As the case of Dora shows, even the sexually open talk of psychoanalytic dialogue has its own unwitting silences. (Billig, 1999, p. 260)

We learn from this beautiful book that when we study silences, we, too, inadvertently reproduce silences. Despite being aware of these limitations, I believe that any particular perspective always makes a contribution that can be discussed and complemented by other perspectives.

I started with an example of Miren Artetxe's and will continue by focusing on the *bertsolaritza* or Basque oral improvisational poetry tradition. The leading bertsolari championship has become so popular in the Basque Country that it attracts thousands of spectators seeking entertainment in the Basque language.

The bertsolaris, or improvisational poet-singers, sometimes express personal opinions in their verses but they also take on different personas, deftly adapting to the themes set by the presenters. The bertsolaris' use of honed rhetorical skills to wax lyrical about their own ideas or defend an opposing idea is reminiscent of classical orators.

The audiences at the live performances identify strongly with the bertsolaris who engage their audiences with a range of rhetorical techniques from humor to gravitas. Like the rhetoricians of ancient Greece, they discuss a range of subjects. They have to be up to date on current affairs because they may be required to argue either side of any issue. During their training, they develop the ability to rhetorically argue all positions on any subject. And the subjects in the competition are always highly topical.

The role of the presenters, or subject-setters, is also highly noteworthy. Ultimately, it involves choosing a subject and a point of view and, in the process, the subject-setters are obliged to take a rhetorical position on the issue and, to some extent, become part of the argument. By studying the art of the bertsolari, we can learn about how ideas are communicated to a large number of people with a shared love of the Basque language. What is said and not said in the performances is also highly significant. Both what is said and what is omitted reflect the ideological atmosphere of the time, and this ideology is created and reproduced in this unique and magnificent form of communication.

So, previously taboo subjects often come up during bertsolari competitions. In this regard, the treatment of gender issues has changed significantly over the last few decades. In the book *Bertsolaritza feminismotik (bir) pentsatzen* ((Re)thinking Bertsolaritza from a Feminist Perspective), the writings and reflections of different authors shed light on this aspect of the oral tradition (Artetxe and Labaka, 2019).

Among the range of bertsolaritza activities, one event stands out: the Bertsolari Championship of the Basque Country. It has a long history and is eagerly awaited every four years. Thousands of Basque speakers travel from town to town, following the qualifying rounds of the competition and attending the final which has taken place at the vast Bilbao Exhibition Center (BEC) since 2005. Several thousands of spectators follow the event either in person or on television. The topics chosen for the championship are fascinating from the point of view of studying the evolution of ideologies. With a view to examining the evolution of the Basque language and identity, I compared the subjects of the verses in the 1980s championships with "what was said and not said" in the 2013 and 2017 finals.

First and foremost, the Basque language is at the heart of the bertsolaritza tradition and, as such, the event is understood to be a pro-Basque language activity. This view is echoed by both bertsolaris and researchers on the subject (Garzia, 2014).

By looking at several examples, Iwill try to illustrate the centrality of the Basque language in the world of Basque improvisational poetry recitals (bertsolaritza). In the 1982 finals in Idiazabal, for example, the bertsolari Sebastian Lizaso sang the following verse[5] in response to the presenter Joxe Mari Iriondo's introductory lead:

Bakar-bakarrik nahi duguna da
euskara salba dadila
sarri askotan eginagatik
alkarrekin korapila
inork ez pentsa heldu geranik
honuntz txapelaren bila
euskeran alde agindu gera
hemen bertsolari pila.

(All we want / is for Basque to be saved. / Although very often / we argue, / let nobody think we have come / to win the prize: / all of us bertsolaris have come / to work in favor of Basque.)

5 Examples of versos sung at the 1982 championsip have been collected by Xenpelar Dokumentazio Zentroa (XDZ), which was created by the cultural association *Bertsozale Elkartea* in 1991 in order to collect, organize and promote the Bertsolaritza´s heritage. The versos used in this book are available at https://bdb.bertsozale.eus

So, it would appear that the most important thing about the bertsolari championship is not who wins but the fact that it is a pro-Basque language initiative. A number of years later, bertsolari Julio Soto sang the following as the farewell at the 2013 Hendaia round of the championship (Bertsozale elkartea & Lanku, 2014, p. 54):

Gaurko helburu hutsa ez zen
puntuz jostea saskia
aldarrikapen bat ere
bazen gaurko arrastia
Hendaiatik Mauleraino
herri baten argazkia
hotz dago Larrun antena
bero Izpegi azpia
Seaskari muxu haundi bat
itxaropenez bustia
segi euskara zabaltzen
irtengo da eguzkia
hizkuntza galtzen bazaigu
galduta dago guztia. (bis)

(Today's goal was not just / to clock up more points, / it was also a proclamation / this afternoon / from Hendaia to Maule, / a photograph of a nation. / The Larrun antenna is cold, / it is hot under Izpegi. / A big kiss for Seaska, / full of hope; / carry on spreading Basque, / the sun will come out. / If we lose our language / all is lost. (bis))

In the '*prison work*' round in the Legazpi leg of the same championship (a 'blind' round where all the competitors compose a verse on the same subject but cannot hear their opponents), Bertsolari Mantxi was asked to recite a verse on the following: "You're glad you make so many people happy." He brought up the Ikastola in Tudela and invited the audience to join in the "Nafarroa Oinez" rally to raise money for the school. So, by referring to "Kilometroak" and "Herri Urrats," he put the Tudela school in the context of the Ikastola movement.

At the 2017 semifinals in Durango, in her first performance Miren Artetxe mentioned the "Errigora" initiative, praised the work of the community, and referred to their dreams. The "Errigora" initiative, which markets food produce from the south of the Basque Country, sends parts of the proceeds to local pro-Basque language initiatives. The importance of the Basque language and associated pro-language initiatives are both recurring themes in the competition.

While the Basque language may be considered a central part of the bertsolaritza discourse, it is important to study the nuances. Hosting pro-Basque language initiatives does not necessarily mean that everyone involved is ideologically aligned in the same way. People can support the Basque language while at the same time hold a very different opinion about its position in relation to Spanish or French.

At the end of the book about the 2013 Bertsolari Championship, Olatz Mitxelena Garmendia provides a reflection. She looks at the choice of themes in the entire competition, and examines the introductions and verses to see how they contribute to the construction of the Basque nationalist identity. She uses a table to summarize the references to politics in the Basque Country, and concludes that the homeland had not been a focal point of the championship that year. Mitxelena attributes this lack of centrality to the context at that time:

> ETA's giving up arms, the release of prisoners, being in work or unemployed, inability to pay the mortgages, the treatment of gender-based violence, the aging population . . . were all issues affecting people's lives and concerns. In fact, the homeland is way down on the list of concerns, even though it seems to have been the number one concern in the Bertsolari Championship finals up to now. (Mitxelena, 2014, p. 403)

Mitxelena Garmendia writes about this transition. She says that people's concerns had changed, suggesting that people were less concerned with the homeland than they had been previously.

When the subject choices of the 1980s' championships are compared with those of the 2013 and 2017 championships, a change in the approach to Basque politics can be seen. Over previous decades when the political situation in the Basque Country had been a leading theme, the perspective reflected in the verses was that of an oppressed nation. Terms such as "oppression" and "enemies" were commonplace, and the power relations of the time were also mentioned. Indeed, the bertsolaris often alluded to the "need for nationalist unity." Examples of this can be seen in the verses sung at the 1982 championship. Jon Enbeita, for instance, sang the following as his final topic when given the theme "We are not right, because there are few of us":

Egia nahikoa da
Katean lotzeko
Edo etsai ihesi
Erbesteratzeko
Zapalkuntza Euskadik

Lepoetan dauko
Arrazoia eskatu
Zigorra ordeko
Arrazoirik ez degu
Gutxi geralako

(The truth is enough / to link to a chain / or to flee from the enemy, / to go into exile. / The Basque Country is oppressed, / right on its neck. / We ask for reason / but get punished instead / We are not right, / because there are few of us.)

In the 1982 championship, several verses referred explicitly to the oppression of the Basque Country and the nationalist unity needed to overcome it. For example, when the presenter Iriondo gave bertsolari Jon Enbeita a topic about seven provinces in a single nation (*zazpi probintzi baina herri bat bakarra*), he came up with the following:

Hori da euskaldunak degun deiadarra
Betiko galdu ez dedin Euskal Herri zaharra
Abertzaleok degu elkartu beharra

(That is the Basques' call / we patriots need to unite / so that the old Basque Country is not lost forever.)

In a competition in Idiazabal in November 1982, when asked to sing on the subject "I am not a fan of war, I am in favor of peace," several bertsolaris connected it to the oppression of the Basque Country and the need for nationalist unity. Lopategi, in the first of his three verses, recited the following:

Bakearen eskaintza
Egiten dute hor
Eta dei horrentzako
Ez nago entzungor
Justizi on batekin
Gura genduke lor
Baldin bagera euskaldun
Baldin anai ta nor
Horretan ahalegin bat
Ez ote dugu zor

(They offer peace / from over there, / and to that call / I am not deaf. / We would like to achieve it / with good justice. / If we are Basque, / if we are brothers, / shouldn't we make / an effort in that direction?)

Zeberio I sang about the subject of war and peace in a way that is virtually unheard-of in public nowadays. He blamed the lack of peace in the Basque Country on those who came to wage war, and invited them to leave the Basque Country:

Neronek nahi nuen gaitxo bat
Orain eman dit neri
Eta bakearen alde ekin
Behar diogu lanari
Eta bala bat sartu buruan
Gerra maite duenari
Bakezaleak izan ta fama
Txarra eman digute guri

Mutur beltz jende zelebre horrek
Andaluzitik aldegin
Bakean zegon gure herriyan

Gerra baten hoiek ekin
Asko etorri dira handikan
Ta inork ez du ahalegin
Pakea hemen jarri nahi bada
Danak bezate aldegin

(I wanted a subject, / I've been given it, / and we have to start work / in favor of peace, / and put a bullet in the head / of he who loves war. / We love peace and / they've given us a bad name. // Those strange, foul-mouthed people / who've come from Andalusia; / we were at peace in our country / they started a war. / Many of them have come here, / and none of them makes an effort. / If we want peace here, / let them all leave.)

At the 1982 championships, when the bertsolaris were given subjects that were not overtly connected to the political situation in the Basque Country, they established a connection. For example, in response to the subject "The red rooster always crows" (*Oilar gandor gorriak beti kukurruku)*, Jon Lopategi sang:

Oilar gandor gorriak
Beti kukurruku
Holako esperientzi
Hamaikatxo dauku
Kanpoko oilar batek
Bait gaitu ikutu
Baina gu ere ez gera
Mantenduko mutu

(The red rooster / always crows, / we have heard him / so many times. / A foreign rooster / has touched us, / but we won't keep / silent either.)

Similar examples can be found as far back as the 1980 championship. Amuriza and Garmendia, for example, when asked to play the role of two birds, with Garmendia in a cage and Amuriza flying free, Amuriza ended a lengthy exchange with this verse (Auspoa, 1980, p. 28):

Eskatzen duzun lan ori ezin
Uka nezake iñola,
Pentsa ala ere gure artean
Zerbait geio badagola;
Askatasuna nik kantatzen dut
Ta zuk sufritzen kaiola,
Bion artean osatzen dugu
Euskalerriko odola

(I can't turn down / that work, no way. / Remember/ there's something more between us too; / I sing for freedom / and you suffer in a cage, / between the two of us / we're the blood of the Basque Country.)

Amuriza also managed to connect the subject "I have pain in my heart" to the political situation in the Basque Country (Auspoa, 1980, p. 35):

Sentimendua sartu zitzaidan
Biotzeraño umetan,
Geroztik ainbat gauza mingarri
Ikusi mundu honetan;
Euskalerriaz batera nago
Biotz barneko penetan:
Anaiak alkar artu eziñik,
Etsaiak su eta ketan,
Esan dudana gezurra bada
Urka nazazue bertan.

Zer kolorezko airea ote
Da gizonaren samiña?
Ni eta zuen barrena ortan
Izan liteke berdiña;
Zoriontsuak izan gintezke
Erri libre bat bagiña,
Baña au ezta orrela eta
Orrek sortzen dit sumiña,
Argatik Balda ontan uzten dut
Nire biotzeko miña

(I had the feeling in my heart, / even as a child. / So many painful things since then, / I have seen in this world. / I am with the Basque Country / in the depth of my heart: / brothers unable to come together, / enemies with fire and flame, / if what I have said is a lie, / let them hang me right now. // What color / is a man's pain? / Inside me and inside you / it could be the same; / we could be happy / if we were a free people, / but that's not the case / and it makes me angry, / that's why I leave the pain in my heart / in this *fronton* court in Balda.)

The bertsolaris of the 1980s were keen to address political issues, and their view of the political situation in the Basque Country reflects that of an oppressed people. A "we" often appears in their verses, and this "we" denotes a patriotic sentiment towards the Basque Country. The "people" and "us," united by the Basque language, is connected with the patriotic "we," the "we" that suffers "oppression." The following verse is taken from the 1980 championship by bertsolari Jon Enbeita in response to the subject set by Iriondo (Auspoa, 1980, p. 20):

Iri: Askoren gaitza degu
Nahi eta ezin
Enb: Ainbat lan era ortan
Euskadin da egin;
Naiz-ta erria jasotzen
Guk betik alegin,
Goikoak indarrakin
Beti du desegin

(Iriondo: We have the disease of many: / we want, but can't. / Enbeita: So much work like this / has been done in the Basque Country: / although we always try, / working from below / It always gets undone / from above)

National oppression and power relations were recurring themes during the decade. The political situation in the Basque Country was very present in these competitions and was introduced by both the organizers and the bertsolaris, who were all keen to bring these themes out into the open.

It is also worth reflecting on the role of the subject-setters. Maite Berriozabal reflects on the importance of the themes set in these competitions in the construction of realities and discourses, in the book *Bertsolaritza feminismotik (bir)pentsatzen* ((Re)thinking Bertsolaritza from a Feminist Perspective). One chapter describes the people who set the subjects and examines their work in the championships and beyond. Depending on the specific circumstances of the event, she examines the degree of power or freedom the subject-setters have to construct a particular discourse or reality. Taking the 2017 championship, for instance, she explains that the process of preparing a championship is a collaborative, highly complex task and adds that all manner of details are measured when deciding on a subject :

> We can say, therefore, that the leading championship has a rigid framework within which the subject-setters must operate. And within this regimented framework, the work of the subject-setting team is based, to a large extent, on attention to detail. (Berriozabal, 2019, p. 184)

Berriozabal shows us how carefully and thoughtfully subjects are set at championships. In this sense, she does not see the role of subject-setters as neutral. She discusses the power of the subject-setters and their ability to influence discourse:

> And the subject will never be objective as the whole design of it is in our hands. We do not control what the bertsolaris create after listening to the subject, but we have the power to mark a direction. Each subject is set for a specific reason and purpose, and sometimes we get what we want, other times we do not, but there is always a chance to have an impact. (Berriozabal, 2019, p. 186)

Subject-setters always look at a number of aspects when examining what they can do with a particular subject. Berriozabal talks about the meaning of words at one point, and also mentions the tone that the subject-setters use when formulating the topics; they can be presented humorously, seriously, or superficially, and all of this makes a difference. She also mentions another key aspect: the subject-setter decides whether or not to set—ultimately, to include or not—a particular theme:

> The subject-setter decides whether or not to set a particular topic. Setting a particular subject makes something, someone or a situation visible, and not setting it means that it does not exist as such. It is another matter whether or not the bertsolaris can build on what has not been said in the subject. (Berriozabal, 2019, p. 186)

This is of particular importance in the subject I am examining here. When the subjects set in the championships of the 1980s are compared with those of the 2013 and 2017 championships, a change in the organizers' willingness to bring up the political situation in the Basque Country is evident. As Olatz Mitxelena points out in her research on the 2013 championship, the subject was clearly being silenced. In 1980 and 1982, the political situation in the Basque Country was a common theme (e.g., topics such as *Seven provinces but only one people*; *Come from abroad and start giving orders*; *We still get beaten for nothing*; *We have sick people in our old country*; *I am not a fan of war, I'm in favor of peace*; and *We are not right because we are few*), but this was no longer the case in 2013 and 2017 when little reference was made to the political situation in the Basque Country. The oppressed people and need for nationalist unity so prevalent in the 1980s had all but disappeared from the list of set themes (Bertsozale elkartea & Lanku, 2014; Bertsozale elkartea & Lanku, 2018).

In his reflections on the 2013 championship, Joxerra Garzia says that the "conflict" was mentioned less than at other times (Garzia, 2014, p. 354). Olatz Mitxelena believes that there was less interest in the political situation (Mitxelena, 2014, p. 403). In order for a subject to disappear from the program it must have been absent from conversations and discourses. If concepts such as "oppression," "an oppressed people," the "unity of nationalists," and "freedom of the Basque Country" are no longer heard, it means that they are falling into disuse. Collectively, and in the same way that Freud and Dora avoided talking about the Jewish question and the political situation of Jews, it seems that the discourse on the Basque language is being separated from the ideology of Basque nationalism by avoiding it. In recent championships, the "we" the Basque language unites is not linked to the "we" united by Basque patriotism.

One could argue, however, that the words of the bertsolaris and the organizers' choice of set subjects are connected with the political situation in the Basque Country, one example potentially being prisoners and imprisonment.

Here again, another point Berriozabal makes about the content of subjects is of special interest. She underlines the enormous importance of how a subject is expressed:

> Setting a subject or making it visible does not always work in favor of the idea behind it. Usually, the way in which a subject is expressed is more important than the subject in itself. (Berriozabal, 2019, p. 186)

At the semifinals of the 2013 championship in Oiartzun, a subject was set for bertsolaris Aitor Sarriegi and Agin Laburu having to do with imprisonment. An examination of the way the subject was presented allows us to see what Berriozabal meant when she mentions how a subject is expressed: "You are a couple, and your relationship began when you were young. After seven years in prison, Agin was released a few months ago. Aitor, today Agin has told you that your relationship is over." This particular formulation highlights a situation which is widespread in the Basque Country: many people have friends or relatives who are political prisoners. Therefore, a political reference is being made, but the way the subject is phrased emphasizes the relationship between the two people rather than the reason for being in prison. The subject Unai Iturriaga was given in the final at Barakaldo also provides us with insight into the nature of the subject. It touches on politics in the Basque Country: "Your father was killed in an attack. This year, for the first time, representatives of all political persuasions attended a memorial ceremony for him." In this case the subject was not set from the point of view of an oppressed people, as it might have been in the eighties: no enemies are mentioned, nor is a nation doomed to fight for its freedom. Through the discourse, to use Berriozabal's words, the subject-setter offers a detailed, non-neutral look at the political situation.

Bertsolaris too have often left out the reason for the incarceration when dealing with the subject of prison or prisoners. Sustrai Colina, for example, at the 2013 Barakaldo finals, when instructed to compose a verse on "The situation has put you on the other side," took on the role of a father who had been imprisoned in the past, and now had to face his feelings as his son was being persecuted politically. In dealing with this subject, emotions and feelings come to the fore. Similar verses were produced by Aitor Sarriegi and Etxahun Lekue in the 2013 championship semi-finals in Donostia, when they were given the following subject: "Your father was in prison when you were born. After serving twenty-five years in prison, he will be released today. You are at the prison gate waiting for him to come out." Both bertsolaris focused on the world of prisoners from the point of view of the family's suffering.

The 2017 championship featured several references to Catalonia. At the time, there was a lot of controversy surrounding the right to decide on their independence. The bertsolaris introduced the issue of the right to decide in several verses. If we compare how Basque politics was treated in the championship in the eighties with how it is treated now, we can see that the discourse has become more individualistic, as I said in chapter six. At the same time, as ideologies include dilemmas, there is controversy in discourse. Although the "group" still exists today, the way it is understood has been evolving since the 1980s.

It is not the purpose of this chapter to carry out an in-depth study of these bertsolaritza competitions. However, I believe that the work of bertsolaris gives us a good insight into the ideology that surrounds the Basque language in the Basque Country. Urla mentioned that pro-Basque language ideology and Basque nationalist ideology have gone hand in hand for years, but by examining the changes in ideology reflected in the bertsolari competitions, it becomes apparent that the "we" united by the Basque language may be ideologically different from the "we" joined by patriotism. For one thing, by placing notions about the Basque language in a broader ideological context, individualistic ideas are expanded, both in the study of the Basque language phenomenon, and in the understanding of Basque politics, as mentioned throughout this book. For another, by examining dilemmas within ideologies, we also encounter the controversy between individualism and collectivism. And we have also seen that the rhetorically created "us" is variable. In the examples mentioned, the fight for the Basque language is not always connected with the nationalist struggle. The nationalist ideology is collectively being silenced and repressed in the same way the Jewish identity was silenced between Freud and Dora.

11. Conclusion

Therefore, the history of the concept of ideology is the history of various attempts to find a firm Archimedean point outside the sphere of ideological discourse, an immovable spot from which to observe the levers of ideology at work.
David McLellan. *Ideology.*

I started this book by emphasizing the importance of context in the analysis of attitudes, ideas, and opinions about the Basque language. As attitudes, ideas, and opinions are situated in an ideological context, I have argued that human thought, and therefore private opinions and ideas, are formed within this context. By placing the individual motivations and attitudes that take center stage in Basque sociolinguistics into their ideological context, I have argued that such attitudes, ideas, and ideologies are themselves rhetorical in nature. I have proposed a new framework for the debate on the future of the Basque language. Rather than understanding psychological processes as driven by individuals' internal impulses, I see them as processes within a context. I have therefore placed attitudes and ideas about the Basque language in the ideological and, hence, rhetorical context of the language.

I do not view the ideology of language as an isolated corpus of ideas; on the contrary, I believe that ideas about language emerge in interaction with ideas about other areas such as politics and science. As I have said throughout this book, humanity lives immersed in a sea of ideologies. The very problematics of ideology arose and developed in close connection with political practice and science (Larrain, 2007, which is why I have prioritized political and scientific context in this work. I have focused on the link between language and national ideologies, and on the complexity of the discursive production of Basque nationality. I have also offered some perceptions about the rhetoric of scientific research on the Basque language, and about the ideological individualism-collectivism controversy which is central to social sciences. Finally, due to the dynamism of ideologies, I have also studied the evolution of discourses on the Basque language, paying special attention to discourses that are silenced.

My aim in this short book is to share an image of the ideological context of the Basque language. As context is dynamic, complex, and continuous, my contribution is a work in progress. Having immersed myself in the world of rhetoric, if anything has become clear to me during this process, it is that the debate is endless. I have shed but a chink of light on what is potentially an infinite subject. These topics, which I have barely touched on, are merely suggestions for a more in-depth analysis of discourse from a rhetorical perspective.

Understanding the rhetorical perspective reminds me that my words, too, are rhetorical. We are constantly adding to our thinking by debating and reasoning through ideologies in context, and this book is just one example of this. I have not, therefore, obtained any "truths" about the social psychology of the Basque language. Nor will we ever. My words and ideas, like everyone else's, are ideological and rhetorical. As I said earlier, there is no escape from rhetoric.

Not having to look for a perfect, neutral "truth" takes a great weight off, but it also leads to other concerns. If we do not have to look for "truth," if all thoughts and ideas are open to debate, if everything is relative, what sense does it make to reflect on any issue? This intellectual tendency, with its suspicion of objective truths, has spread across Western academic knowledge and taken on many different names:

> The unifying perspective of this movement has variously been called social constructionism, the rhetorical turn, society as a text, deconstructionism and postmodernism. (Harvey Brown, 1994, p. 13)

Apart from the development of this intellectual tendency, the concerns I mentioned have also spread among postmodern intellectuals. As Herbert W. Simons and Michael Billig argue, the problem is not that the postmodernist spirit lacks a critical impulse, but that critique is running rampant without political direction. They point to an important problem we are facing with regard to ideological criticism:

> If ideology critique is criticized for believing in "true" political principles, will this result in a conservative acceptance of ideological forces? Should not radical politics put a firm fence around the critical impulse in order to limit its anarchic impulses? (Billig & Simons, 1994, p. 6)

How can you point out social injustices if arguments can be made for and against them rhetorically, and if one is not "truer" than the other? And what if the very concept of "injustice" is rhetorical? Reflecting on this leads us to different authors' thoughts and arguments, which, in turn, add to the difficulty of reaching a single conclusion. And so, the process goes on and on. One can continue to ask questions without ever finding a satisfactory solution.

Not all authors who favor the rhetorical approach, however, reflect on "truth" in the same way. As Simons said, there is no single rhetoric of inquiry, and the study of research rhetoric is not explicitly limited to studies that fall within the subject area; a number of researchers and research projects exist which are implicitly included in the rhetorical approach without being explicitly labelled as such (Simons, 1990a). What I mean by this is that the "world" of rhetoric is vast and that not all authors can be grouped together in one category; those who make the sharpest criticism of realism hold that rhetoric is the only thing that exists (de Man, 1978), while others argue that rhetoric should be treated in conjunction with objectivist philosophy, leaving open the possibility of making compatible the two points of view (Keith and Cherwitz, 1989).

Rather than examining any deeper these broader issues, I have tried to shine some light on the ideological context of the Basque language. The approach I have used, which argues that the psychology of individuals cannot be separated from the context, is a rhetorical position. It is a way of understanding human psychology and thought, and it is the stance I have taken in the ideological debate on individualism-collectivism referred to throughout the book.

Likewise, if ideologies are rhetorical, the power that is exercised through institutionalized behavior, too, is an evolving rhetorical process. Arguments and counter-arguments can be made when examining an issue, and ideological processes based on controversy will go one way or another depending on the level of institutionalization. As the poet Joseba Sarrionandia says, in this twilight disorder, each landscape is representative of all possible landscapes, and this life is representative of all possible lives (*iluntzeko desordu honetan, paisaia bakoitza, paisaia possible guztien ordezkaria, eta bizitza hau, bizitza possible guztien ordezkaria*) (Sarrionandia, 2013).

On the subject of nationalism, my question is not whether good and bad nationalisms exist. Depending on the level of institutionalization of any particular nationalism, there are differences among more and less consolidated nations. I consider nationalism to be weaker or stronger as a social process. I take the same view on ideologies in general. Since all ideologies are rhetorical, I have not claimed that some are "truer" than others.

But among ideologies, as among nations, there are differences according to the degree of consolidation, depending on the level of institutionalization. The higher the level of institutionalization, the "truer" the ideas seem. And whether they are "truths" or not, I believe that the dynamism of ideologies and the power relations between them condition social phenomena. Recalling Therborn's view on the subject, like the confusion caused by noise and light in a big city, the ideologies of the Basque language are constructed and deconstructed through a process of continual interaction and collision.

References:

Abrams, J. R., Barker, V., & Giles, H. (2009). An examination of the validity of the subjective vitality questionnaire. *Journal of Multilingual and Multicultural Development, 30*, 59-72.

Abric, J. C. (1984). A theoretical and experimental approach to the study of social representations in a situation of interaction. In R. M. Farr, & S. Moscovici (Eds.), *Social representations* (pp. 169-184). Cambridge University Press.

Adam, I. (2013). Immigrant integration policies of the Belgian regions: Sub-state nationalism and policy divergence after devolution. *Regional and Federal Studies, 23*, 547-569.

Albarracín, D., & Vargas, P. (2010). Attitudes and persuasion: From biology to social responses to persuasive intent. In S. T. Fiske, D. T. Gilbert, & G. Lindzey (Eds.), *Handbook of social psychology* (pp. 394-427). John Wiley & Sons Inc.

Anderson, B. (1983). *Comunidades imaginadas. Reflexiones sobre el origen y la difusión del nacionalismo* [Imagined Communities. Reflections on the Origin and Spread of Nationalism] (E. L. Suárez Trans.). México: Fondo de Cultura Económica.

Ariznabarreta, J. (2007). *Pueblo y poder. Cuadernos para la reconstrucción de la razón*. Zarautz: Self-published.

Ariznabarreta, L. (2019). *Notes on Basque culture. The aftermath of epics*. Uruguay: Biblioteca Euskal Erria. Universidad CLAEH.

Arnberg, L. N., & Arnberg, P. W. (1992). Language awareness and language separation. *Cognitive Processing in Bilinguals, 83*, 475-500.

Artetxe, M., & Labaka, A. (Eds.). (2019). *Bertsolaritza feminismotik (bir)pentsatzen*. Bilbo: UEU.

Auspoa. (1980). *Bertsolari txapelketa nagusia (Donostia, 1980-1-6)*. Tolosa: Auspoa.

Azurmendi, M. J., Larrañaga, N., & Apalategi, J. (2008). Bilingualism, identity, and citizenship in the Basque Country. In M. Nino-Murcia, & J. Rothman (Eds.), *Bilingualism and identity: Spanish at the crossroads with other languages* (pp. 56-63). Amsterdam: John Benjamins.

Azurmendi, M. J., & Martínez de Luna, I. (2011). Success-failure continuum of Euskara in the Basque Country. In J. A. Fishman, & O. Garcia (Eds.), *Handbook of language and ethnic identity. Vol 2: The success-failure continuum in language and ethnic identity efforts* (pp. 323-335). New York: Oxford University Press.

Barker, F. (2010). Learning to be a majority: Negotiating immigration, integration and national membership in Quebec. *Political Science, 62*(1), 11-36.

Berger, P. L., & Luckmann, T. (1967). *The social construction of reality*. New York: Doubleday Anchor.

Berriozabal, M. (2019). Gaien garrantzia errealitate eta diskurtsoen eraikuntzan. In M. Artetxe, & A. Labaka (Eds.), *Bertsolaritza feminismotik (bir) pentsatzen* (pp. 181-201). Bilbo: UEU.

Berthod, O. (2016). Institutional theory of organizations. *Global encyclopedia of public administration, public policy, and governance* (pp. 1-5). Springer International Publishing AG.

Bertsozale elkartea, & Lanku. (2014). *Bertsolari txapelketa nagusia 2013*. Andoain: Euskal Herriko bertsozale elkartea and Lanku.

Bertsozale elkartea & Lanku. (2018). *Bertsolari txapelketa nagusia 2017*. Andoain: Bertsozale elkartea andLanku.

Billig, M. (1987). *Arguing and thinking. A rhetorical approach to social psychology*. Cambridge: Cambridge University Press.

Billig, M. (1988). The notion of 'prejudice': Some rhetorical and ideological aspects. *Text*, 8, 91-110.

Billig, M. (1990). Collective memory, ideology and the British royal family. *Collective remembering* (pp. 60-80). London: SAGE.

Billig, M. (1991). *Ideology and opinions*. London: SAGE.

Billig, M. (1993). Studying the thinking society: Social representations, rhetoric and attitudes. In G. M. Breakwell, & D. V. Canter (Eds.), *Empirical approaches to social representations* (pp. 39-62). Clarendon Press/Oxford University Press.

Billig, M. (1995). *Banal nationalism.* London: SAGE Publications.

Billig, M. (1999). *Freudian repression. Conversation creating the unconscious.* United Kingdom: Cambridge University Press.

Billig, M. (2008). Social representations and repression: Examining the first formulations of Freud and Moscovici. *Journal for the Theory of Social Behavior, 38*(4), 355-368.

Billig, M. (2009). Discursive psychology, rhetoric and the issue of agency. *Semen, 27*, 2020.

Billig, M. (2017). Banal nationalism and the imagining of politics. In M. Skey, & M. Antonsich (Eds.), *Everyday nationhood. Theorising culture, identity and belonging after banal nationalism* (pp. 307-321). London. United Kingdom: Palgrave-Macmillan.

Billig, M., Condor, S., Edwards, D., Gane, M., Middleton, D., & Radley, A. (1988). *Ideological dilemmas. A social psychology of everyday thinking.* London: SAGE.

Billig, M., & Marinho, C. (2017). *The politics and rhetoric of commemoration.* Great Britain: Bloomsbury Academic.

Billig, M., & Simons, H. W. (1994). Introduction. In H. W. Simons, & M. Billig (Eds.), *After postmodernism* (pp. 1-11). London: SAGE.

Blommaert, J., & Verschueren, J. (1998). The role of language in European nationalist ideologies. In B. B. Schieffelin, K. A. Woolard, & P. V. Kroskrity (Eds.), *Language ideologies. Practice and theory* (pp. 189-210). Oxford: Oxford University Press.

Bourhis, R. Y., Giles, H., & Rosenthal, D. (1981). Notes on construction of a 'subjective vitality questionnaire' for ethnolinguistic groups. *Journal of Multilingual and Multicultural Development, 2*, 145-155.

Bourhis, R. Y., & Sachdev, I. (1984). Vitality perceptions and language attitudes: Some Canadian data. *Journal of Language and Social Psychology, 3*(2), 97-127.

Brown, D. (1999). Are there good and bad nationalisms? *Nations and Nationalism, 5*(2), 281-302.

Byram, M. (1997). 'Cultural awareness' as vocabulary learning. *The Language Learning Journal, 16*(1), 51-57.

Byram, M. (2012). Language awareness and (critical) cultural awareness—relationships, comparisons and contrasts. *Language Awareness, 21*(1-2), 5-13.

Calhoun, C. (2017). The rhetoric of nationalism. In M. Skey, & M. Antonsich (Eds.), *Everyday nationhood. Theorising culture, identity and belonging after banal nationalism* (pp. 17-30). London. United Kingdom: Palgrave-Macmillan.

Campion, A. (1923). *Narraciones baskas*. Madrid: CALPE.

Cenoz, J., & Valencia, J. F. (1993). Ethnolinguistic vitality, social networks and motivation in second language acquisition: Some data from the Basque Country. *Language, Culture and Curriculum*, 6(2), 113-127.

Cudd, A. E. (2006). *Analyzing oppression*. New York: Oxford University Press.

Czubaroff, J. (1989). The deliberative character of strategic scientific debates. In H. W. Simons (Ed.), *Rhetoric in the human sciences* (pp. 28-47). London: SAGE.

David, E. J. R. (Ed.). (2014). *Internalized oppression. The psychology of marginalized groups*. New York: Springer Publishing Company.

David, E. J. R., & Derthick, A. O. (2014). What is internalized oppression, and so what? In E. J. R. David (Ed.), *Internalized oppression. The psychology of marginalized groups* (pp. 1-30). New York: Springer Publishing Company.

de Man, P. (1978). The epistemology of metaphor. *Critical Inquiry*, 5(1), 13-30.

Decker, H. S. (1999). *Freud, Dora y la Viena de 1900* [Freud, Dora and Vienna 1900] (B. Hopkins Trans.). Madrid: Biblioteca Nueva.

Eagly, A. H., & Chaiken, S. (2005). Attitude research in the 21st century: The current state of knowledge. In D. Albarracín, B. T. Johnson, & M. P. Zanna (Eds.),

The handbook of attitudes (pp. 743-767). Lawrence Erlbaum.

Echeverria, B. (2005). Language attitudes in San Sebastian: The Basque vernacular as challenge to Spanish language hegemony. *Journal of Multilingual and Multicultural Development,* 26(3), 249-264.

Edwards, D. (2012). Discursive and scientific psychology. *British Journal of Social Psychology, 51,* 425-435.

Edwards, D., & Middleton, D. (1988). Conversational remembering and family relationships: How children learn to remember. *Journal of Social and Personal Relationships, 5,* 3-25.

Ehala, M. (2009). An evaluation matrix for ethno-linguistic vitality. In S. Pertot, T. Priestly, & C. Williams (Eds.), *Rights, promotion and integration issues for minority languages in Europe* (pp. 123-137). Hampshire, NY: Palgrave-Macmillan.

Eisenstadt, S. N. (1968). Social institutions: The concept. In D. L. Sills (Ed.), *International encyclopedia of the social sciences* (pp. 409-421). New York: Macmillan.

Elexpuru, J. M. (2018). *¿Qué está pasando con Iruña-Veleia?* Navarra: Pamiela.

Erize, X. (2003). History of the Basque language: From the discourse of its death to its maintenance. In M. J. Azurmendi, & I. Martínez de Luna (Eds.), *The case of Basque: Past, present and future* (pp. 19-41). Donostia: Soziolinguistika klusterra.

Errington, J. (1998). Indonesian('s) development: On the state of a language of state. In B. B. Schieffelin, K. A. Woolard, & P. V. Kroskrity (Eds.), *Language ideologies. Practice and theory* (pp. 271-284). Oxford: Oxford University Press.

Fairclough, N. (1992). *Discourse and social change.* Cambridge, UK: Polity Press.

Ferguson, M. J., & Fukukura, J. (2012). Likes and dislikes: A social cognitive perspective on attitudes. In S. T. Fiske, & C. N. Macrae (Eds.), *The SAGE handbook of social cognition* (pp. 165-190). Thousand Oaks, CA: SAGE.

Fiske, S. T., & Taylor, S. E. (2013). *Social cognition. From brains to culture.* London: SAGE.

Fraser, C. (1994). Attitudes, social representations and widespread beliefs. *Papers on Social Representations-Textes Sur Les Représentations Sociales, 3*(1), 1-138.

Friedland, R., & Alford, R. R. (1991). Bringing society back in: Symbols, practices, and institutional contradictions. In W. W. Powell, & P. J. DiMaggio (Eds.), *The new institutionalism in organizational analysis* (pp. 232-263). USA: The University of Chicago Press.

Gal, S., & Irvine, J. T. (1995). The boundaries of languages and disciplines: How ideologies construct difference. *Social Research, 62*(4), 967-1001.

Garzia, J. (2014). Litekeenetik baiezkora (finalaren aitzakian). *Bertsolari txapelketa nagusia 2013* (pp. 351-357). Bertsozale Elkartea-Lanku.

Giacopuzzi, G. (1997). *ETA p.m., el otro camino*. Tafalla (Nafarroa): Txalaparta.

Giles, H., Bourhis, R. Y., & Taylor, D. M. (1977). Towards a theory of language in ethnic group relations. In H. Giles (Ed.), *Language, ethnicity and intergroup relations* (pp. 307-348). London: Academic Press.

Giles, H., & Ogay, T. (2007). Communication accommodation theory. In B. B. Whaley, & W. Samter (Eds.), *Explaining communication: Contemporary theories and exemplars* (pp. 293-310). Mahwah, NJ: Lawrence Erlbaum.

Giles, H., Taylor, D. M., & Bourhis, R. Y. (1973). Towards a theory of interpersonal accommodation through speech: Some Canadian data. *Language in Society, 2*, 177-192.

Gill, R. (2014). An ideological dilemma. The resurgence of sexism and the disappearance of 'sexism.' In C. Antaki, & S. Condor (Eds.), *Rhetoric, ideology and social psychology* (pp. 109-121). Oxfordshire: Routledge.

Guendouzi, J., & Müller, N. (2006). *Approaches to discourse in dementia*. Mahwah, New Jersey: Lawrence Erlbaum Associates, Publishers.

Hamilton, H. E. (2008). Language and dementia: Sociolinguistic aspects. *Annual Review of Applied Linguistics, 28*, 91-110.

Harvey Brown, R. (1994). Reconstructing social theory after the postmodern critique. In H. W. Simons, & M. Billig (Eds.), *After postmodernism* (pp. 12-37). London: SAGE.

Haugen, E. (1966). Dialect, language, nation. *American Anthropologist, 68*(4), 922-935.

Hepburn, E. (2009). Regionalist party mobilisation on immigration. *West European Politics, 32*, 514-535.

Howitt, D. (2010). *Introduction to qualitative research methods in psychology. Putting theory into practice.* United Kingdom: Pearson.

Husband, C., & Saifullah Khan, V. (1982). The viability of ethnolinguistic vitality some creative doubts. *Journal of Multilingual and Multicultural Development, 3*(3), 193-205.

Hutchinson, J. (2006). Hot and banal nationalism: The nationalization of the masses. In G. Delanty, & K. Kumar (Eds.), *The SAGE handbook of nations and nationalism* (pp. 295-306). London: SAGE.

Iriarte, I. (2000). El legado de los éuskaros: El discurso sobre el euskara en el "suplemento" en vascuence de príncipe de viana. In R. Jimeno (Ed.), *El euskera en tiempo de los éuskaros* (pp. 317-338). Gobierno de Navarra, Dirección General de Universidades y Política Lingüística.

Irvine, J., & Gal, S. (2000). Language ideology and linguistic differentiation. In P. Kroskrity (Ed.), *Regimes of language: Ideologies, polities and identities* (pp. 35-83). Santa Fe, N.M.: School of American Research Press.

Israel, J., & Tajfel, H. (Eds.). (1972). *The context of social psychology*. London: Academic Press.

Iza, I. (2010). *Ikastola mugimendua: Dabilen herria*. Bilbo: Jagon Saila: Euskaltzaindia.

Jack, J., & Appelbaum, G. (2010). This is your brain on rhetoric: Research directions for neurorhetorics. *Rhetoric Society Quarterly, 40*(5), 411-437.

Jaspars, J. M. F., & Fraser, C. (1984). Attitudes and social representations. In R. M. Farr, & S. Moscovici (Eds.), *Social representations* (pp. 104-124). Paris: Presses Universitaires de France.

Jáuregui, G. (1981). *Ideología y estrategia política de ETA: Análisis de su evolución entre 1959 y 1968*. Madrid: Siglo XXI.

Jepperson, R. L. (1991). Institutions, institutional effects, and institutionalism. In W. W. Powell, & P. J. DiMaggio (Eds.), *The new institutionalism in organizational analysis* (pp. 143-163). USA: The University of Chicago Press.

Jeram, S. (2013). Immigrants and the Basque nation: Diversity as a new marker of identity. *Ethnic and Racial Studies, 36*, 1770-1788.

Jeram, S. (2016). Looking forward into the past: *Partido Nacionalista Vasco* and the immigrant question in the Basque Country. *Journal of Ethnic and Migration Studies, 42*(8), 1257-1270.

Jeram, S., & Adam, I. (2015). Diversity and nationalism in the Basque Country and Flanders: Understanding immigrants as fellow minorities. *National Identities, 17*(3), 241-257.

Jones, R., & Merriman, P. (2009). Hot, banal and everyday nationalism: Bilingual road signs in Wales. *Political Geography, 28*(3), 164-173.

Keith, W. M., & Cherwitz, R. A. (1989). Objectivity, disagreement and the rhetoric of inquiry. In H. W. Simons (Ed.), *Rhetoric in the human sciences* (pp. 195-210). London: SAGE.

Kinder, D. R., & Sears, D. O. (1981). Prejudice and politics: Symbolic racism versus racial threats to the good life. *Journal of Personality and Social Psychology, 40*(3), 414-431.

Krasner, S. D. (1993). Westphalia and all that. In J. Goldstein, & R. Keohane (Eds.), *Ideas and foreign policy* (pp. 235-264). Ithaca, NY: Cornell University Press.

Kymlicka, W. (2001). *Politics in the vernacular: Nationalism, multiculturalism, and citizenship*. New York, NY: Oxford University Press.

Larrain, J. (2007). *El concepto de ideología. vol. 1. Carlos Marx*. Santiago de Chile, Chile: LOM.

Larrañaga, N., Garcia I., Azurmendi, M. J., & Bourhis, R. (2016). Identity and acculturation: Interethnic relations in the Basque Autonomous Community. *Journal of Multilingual and Multicultural Development, 37*(2), 131-149.

Lasagabaster, D. (2005). Attitudes towards Basque, Spanish and English: An analysis of the most influential variables. *Journal of Multilingual and Multicultural Development, 26*(4),296-316.

Lasagabaster, D., & Sierra, J. M. (2009). Language attitudes in CLIL and traditional EFL classes. *International CLIL Research Journal, 1*(2), 4-17.

Law, A. (2001). Near and far: Banal national identity and the press in Scotland. *Media, Culture & Society,* 23 (3), 299-317.

Liddicoat, A. J., & Taylor-Leech, K. (2015). Multilingual education: The role of language ideologies and attitudes. *Current Issues in Language Planning, 16*(1-2), 1-7.

Lindblom, C. E. (1977). *Politics and markets: The world's political-economic systems*. New York: Basic Books.

Lopez-Antón, J. J. (2010). *Arturo Campión entre la historia y la cultura*. Navarra: Gobierno de Navarra.

Lukes, S. (1971). The meanings of "individualism." *Journal of the History of Ideas, 32*(1), 45-66.

Lukes, S. (2005). *Power. A radical view.* (2nd ed.). London, UK: Palgrave Macmillan.

MacInnes, J., Rosie, M., Petersoo, P., Condor, S., & Kennedy, J. (2007). Where is the British national press? *The British Journal of Sociology, 58*(2), 185-206.

McConahay, J. B., & Hough, J. C. (1976). Symbolic racism. *Journal of Social Issues, 32*(2), 23-45.

McKinlay, A., & McVittie, C. (2008). *Social psychology and discourse*. UK: Wiley-Blackwell.

McLellan, D. (1995). *Ideology*. Minneapolis. USA: University of Minnesota Press.

Middleton, D., & Edwards, D. (Eds.). (1990a). *Collective remembering*. London: SAGE.

Middleton, D., & Edwards, D. (1990b). Introduction. In D. Middleton, & D. Edwards (Eds), *Collective remembering* (pp. 1-22). London: SAGE.

Mitxelena, O. (2014). Hitzaren jolasa, zeren eraikuntza? *Bertsolari txapelketa nagusia 2013* (pp. 401-403). Bertsozale elkartea-Lanku.

Moi, T. (1981). Representation of patriarchy: Sexuality and epistemology in Freud's Dora. *Feminist Review, 9*, 60-74.

Moscovici, S. (1963). Attitudes and opinions. *Annual Review of Psychology, 14*, 231-260.

Moscovici, S. (1984). The phenomenon of social representations. In R. M. Farr, & S. Moscovici (Eds.), *Social representations*. Cambridge, UK: Cambridge University Press.

Moscovici, S. (2008). *Psychoanalysis. Its image and its public*. Cambridge, UK: Polity Press.

Odriozola, J. M. (2017). *Nora goaz euskalduntasun honekin?* Donostia: Elkar.

Perelman, C., & Olbrechts-Tyteca, L. (1969). *The new rhetoric. A treatise on argumentation*. USA: University of Notre Dame Press.

Potter, J., & Wetherell, M. (1987). *Discourse and social psychology. Beyond attitudes and behaviour*. London: SAGE.

Ramas, M. (1980). Freud's Dora, Dora's hysteria: The negation of a Woman's rebellion. *Feminist Studies, 6*(3), 472-510.

Ridge, S. G. M., Makoni, S., & Ridge, E. (2003). I want to be like a human again. Morbidity and retained ability in an Alzheimer sufferer. *AILA Review, 16*(1), 149-169.

Romay, J., Garcia-Mira, R., & Azurmendi, M. J. (1999). Ethnolinguistic identity and ethnolinguistic vitality in the bilingual autonomous communities of Spain. *Revista De Psicologia Social, 14*(1), 87-106.

Rosie, M., MacInnes, J., Petersoo, P., Condor, S., & Kennedy, J. (2004). Nation speaking unto nation? National identity and the press in the developed UK. *Sociological Review, 52*, 437-458.

Rumelhart, D. E. (1980). Schemata: The building blocks of cognition. In R. J. Spiro, B. C. Bruce, & W. F. Brewer (Eds.), *Theoretical issues in reading comprehension* (pp. 33-49). Hillsdale: Lawrence Erlbaum Associates.

Sarrionandia, J. (2013). *Hnuy Illa Nyha Majah Yahoo. Poemak (1985-1995)*. Donostia: Elkar.

Sayers, J. (1990). *Sigmund Freud: The basics.* Routledge.

Schieffelin, B. B., Woolard, K. A., & Kroskrity, P. V. (1998). *Language ideologies. Practice and theory.* Oxford: Oxford University Press.

Schneider, D. (1976). Notes toward a theory of culture. In K. M. Basso, & H. L. Silby (Eds.), *Meaning in anthropology* (pp. 197-220). Albuquerque: University of New Mexico Press.

Scott, W. R. (2014). *Institutions and organizations. Ideas, interests, and identities* (4th edition). London, UK: SAGE Publications Ltd.

Sherif, M., & Hovland, C. I. (1961). *Social judgment: Assimilation and contrast effects in communication and attitude change.* New Haven, CT: Yale University Press.

Simons, H. W. (1990a). The rhetoric of inquiry as an intellectual movement. *The rhetorical turn* (pp. 1-31). Chicago: The University of Chicago Press.

Simons, H. W. (1990b). *The rhetorical turn.* Chicago: The University of Chicago Press.

Simons, H. W. (2014). Billig on rhetoric. In C. Antaki, & S. Condor (Eds.), *Rhetoric, ideology and social psychology. Essays in honour of Michael Billig* (pp. 17-28). Oxfordshire: Routledge.

Skey, M. (2009). The national in everyday life: A critical engagement with Michael Billig's thesis of *banal nationalism. The Sociological Review, 57*(2), 331-346.

Skey, M., & Antonsich, M. (Eds.). (2017). *Everyday nationhood. Theorising culture, identity and belonging after banal nationalism*. London. United Kingdom: Palgrave-Macmillan.

Soares, C. (2018). The philosophy of individualism: A critical perspective. *International Journal of Philosophy and Social Values, 1*(1), 11-34.

Spasić, I. (2017). The universality of banal nationalism, or can the flag hang unobtrusively outside a Serbian post office? In M. Skey, & M. Antonsich (Eds.), *Everyday nationhood. Theorising culture, identity and belonging after banal nationalism* (pp. 31-51). London, UK: Palgrave Macmillan.

Streeck, W., & Schmitter, P. C. (1985). Community, market, state-and associations? The prospective contribution of interest governance to social order. In W. Streeck, & P. C. Schmitter (Eds.), *Private interest government: Beyond market and state* (pp. 1-29). Beverly Hills, CA: Sage.

Tajfel, H. (1972). Introduction. In J. Israel, & H. Tajfel (Eds.), *The context of social psychology* (pp. 1-13). London: Academic Press.

Tajfel, H. (1974). Social identity and intergroup behavior. *Social Science Information, 13*, 65-93.

Therborn, G. (1980). *The ideology of power and the power of ideology*. London: Verso.

Thompson, J. B. (1984). *Studies in the theory of ideology*. Cambridge, UK: Polity Press.

Tolbert, P. S., & Zucker, L. G. (1996). The institutionalization of institutional theory. In S. R. Clegg, C. Hardy, & W. R. Nord (Eds.), *Handbook of organization studies* (pp. 175-190). London: SAGE.

Tollefson, J. W. (1991). *Planning language, planning inequality*. Longman.

Tomasello, M. (1999). *The cultural origins of human cognition*. USA: Harvard University Press.

Tomasello, M. (2010). *Origins of human communication*. Cambridge: MIT Press.

Tomasello, M., Dweck, C., Silk, J., Skyrms, B., & Spelke, E. (2009). *Why we cooperate*. USA: MIT Press.

Torrealdai, J. M. (1982). Euskararen zapalkuntza (1936-1939). *Jakin, 24*, 5-73.

Toulmin, S. (1972). *Human understanding, volume I: The collective use and evolution of concepts*. Princeton University Press.

Tulving, E. (1972). Episodic and semantic memory. In E. Tulving, & W. Donaldson (Eds.), *Organization of memory* (pp. 381-403). New York: Academic Press.

Urla, J. (2012). *Reclaiming Basque. Language, nation, and cultural activism*. Reno, Nevada. USA: University of Nevada Press.

Urla, J., & Burdick, C. (2018). Counting matters: Quantifying the vitality and value of Basque. *International Journal of the Sociology of Language*. 252, 73-96.

Verba, S., & Orren, G. R. (1985). The meaning of equality in America. *Political Science Quarterly, 100*(3), 369-387.

Vygotsky, L. S. (1929). The problem of the cultural development of the child. *Journal of Genetic Psychology, 36*, 415-434.

Weber, M. (1975). *El político y el científico*. Madrid: Alianza.

Wertsch, J. V. (1987). Collective memory: Issues from a socio-historical perspective. *Quarterly Newsletter of the Laboratory of Comparative Human Cognition, 9*(1), 19-22.

Williams, T. K. (2012). *Understanding internalized oppression: A theoretical conceptualization of internalized subordination. Open Access Dissertations*. 627.

Wolpaw, J. R. (2002). Memory in neuroscience: Rhetoric versus reality. *Behavioral and Cognitive Neuroscience Reviews, 1*(2), 130-163.

Woolard, K. A. (1998). Introduction. Language ideology as a field of inquiry. In B. B. Schieffelin, K. A. Woolard, & P. V. Kroskrrity (Eds.), *Language ideologies. Practice and theory* (pp. 3-47). Oxford: Oxford University Press.

Yagmur, K., & Ehala, M. (2011). Tradition and innovation in the ethnolinguistic vitality theory. *Journal of Multilingual and Multicultural Development, 32*(2), 101-110.

Zabaleta-Imaz, I. (2000). *Nazioa eta hezkuntza-sistema espainiarraren sorrera*. Bilbo: UEU.

Zucker, L. G. (1983). Organizations as institutions. In S. B. Bacharach (Ed.), (pp. 1-47). Greenwich, CT: JAI Press.

www.ingramcontent.com/pod-product-compliance
Lightning Source LLC
LaVergne TN
LVHW090949080826
845145LV00003B/942

* 9 7 8 1 9 4 9 8 0 5 6 9 7 *